Acknowledgments

This second edition of From Library Skills to Information Literacy is, like its predecessors, a collaborative effort. Over a period of several years, many people have been involved in the thinking and sharing of ideas and resources. It is with gratitude and appreciation that we acknowledge them. Each of the following people had key roles in shaping the direction of this publication:

    Christina Doyle, Director of Learning Technologies, Kern County Office of Education
    Marsha Korobkin, Program Manager, San Diego City Schools
    Ann Lathrop, Professor, California State University, Long Beach
    Joyce Roth, Education Consultant
    Sandy Schuckett, Library Media Teacher, El Sereno Middle School, Los Angeles Unified School District

Several education agencies and professional associations have been instrumental in sharing resources and providing welcome support. The efforts of all these collaborators are greatly appreciated.

    California Association for Bilingual Education
    California Department of Education
    California School Library Association (Special thanks to Christine Allen and Bonnie O'Brian)
    Colorado Department of Education
    LEP Instructional Materials Planning Committee, Los Angeles County Office of Education
    Pullias Reference Center, Los Angeles County Office of Education
    Washington Office of Superintendent of Public Instruction

This second edition is a merger of the first edition and of the interim working paper, *Information Literate in Any Language*. Diane Berthoin-Hernandez did much of the cutting, pasting, and interweaving necessary to make a new whole.

Finally, collaboration and project development also required coordination, leadership, and task masters, roles which were assumed by:

    Zhita Rea, Consultant-in-charge, Library and Media Services, Los Angeles County Office of Education

    David V. Loertscher, Professor, School of Library and Information Science, San Jose State University

Preface

This second edition of the handbook, *From Library Skills to Information Literacy*, has a history that, in some ways, reflects its major themes. It is a collaborative work that includes the thinking of library media specialists, bilingual coordinators, technology leaders, and classroom teachers. It has evolved from previous works:

- *Research as a Process: Developing Skills for Life in an Information Society* (1989) "began with a small group of high school librarians who wanted to prepare students for on-line database searching" and eventually realized that "everyone needed a new way to think about information."

- *From Library Skills to Information Literacy: A Handbook for the 21st Century* (1994) built on and refined the earlier research process model to include the thinking of Kuhlthau, Eisenberg and Berkowitz, Stripling and Pitts, and others who were all considering new ways to explore the wildly exploding worlds of information.

- *Information Literate in Any Language* (1995) appeared as a working paper and supplement to *From Library Skills to Information Literacy*. Its mission was to ensure that learners of all languages are included as the focus for instructional planning to develop information literacy. It confirms the obvious, but often overlooked, concept that the need for information literacy is both universal and language dependent; it applies to any – and all – languages.

The present publication is a synthesis, and an extension, of all its predecessors.

- It expands the focus on collaborative planning to include bilingual, ESL, technology and specialists.

- It expands the discussion and provides more examples of instructional strategies that support the development of information literacy.

- It acknowledges and emphasizes the backgrounds and experiences – languages, homes, and communities – of all students.

- It acknowledges and compares both traditional and constructivist teaching and learning.

Finally, although the bits and bytes of information increase exponentially and the sophistication and extension of information access continue to amaze, the basic premise of this and each of the preceding publications remains the same: the need for information is universal and the quest for information is problem-solving based on critical thinking.

From Library Skills to Information Literacy:

A Handbook for the 21st Century

2nd Edition

California School Library Association

1997
Hi Willow Research and Publishing
Castle Rock, Colorado

Suggested Cataloging:

California School Library Association
    From library skills to information literacy : a handbook for the 21st century / California School Library Association. — 2nd ed. — Castle Rock, Colo.: Hi Willow Research and Publishing, 1997.
        vii, 153p. ; 22x28 cm.

    The first edition was published by the same organization under the name: California Media and Library Educators Association in 1994.

    1. Information retrieval. 2. Searching, Bibliographical.
3. Research - Methodology. I. Title

025.524 -dc20

Copyright © 1997 California School Library Association
All Rights Reserved
Printed in the United States of America

This publication can be used by schools and districts with recognition as the basis of local information skills documents without seeking permission of the copyright holder. However, materials in this publication drawn from other copyrighted sources retain their original copyrights and formal permission must be sought if the item is reprinted. If material from this handbook is to be sold, written permission must be sought through the publisher from the Association.

Hi Willow Research and Publishing
P.O. Box 720268
San Jose, CA 95172-0268

Distributed by:
LMC Source
P.O. Box 266
Castle Rock, CO 80104
800-873-3043

ISBN: 0-931510-49-X

Table of Contents

Introductory Materials
    Acknowledgments v
    Preface vi
    Introduction vii

Chapter 1
    Schooling for an Information Society 1
        Information in Today's World 2
        Notes 6

Chapter 2
    Information Literacy: a definition 7
        Information Literacy 8
        The Searcher's Thinking 10
        The Search Process 11
        The Instructional Strategies 12
        The Information Literacy Model Summary 13
        From Library Skills to Information Literacy: New Approaches 15
        Developing Your Own Information Literacy Model 15
        Notes 17

Chapter 3
    The Search Process: Searcher Behaviors and Competencies 19
        The Search Process 20
        The Search Process: Searcher Behaviors and Competencies....................21
        Notes 28

Chapter 4
    Instructional Planning for Information Literacy: A Team Approach 29
        A Team Approach to Information Literacy..30
        Planning Approaches: Traditional and Constructivist 31
        Collaborative Planning of Traditional Units 33
        Collaboration to Create a Constructivist Unit 36
        Collaboration for Improved Academic Achievement 38
        Designing Units: Traditional and Constructivist 38
        Assessing Teaching and Learning 45
        Notes 47

Chapter 5
    The Instructional Process: Resource-Based Learning....................................49
        Resource-Based Learning 50
        Resources in the Home, Community, School, and Beyond......................53
        Learning Resources: People, Places, Print, Technology 58
        Notes 70

Information Literacy

Chapter 6
  The Instructional Process: Strategies for Developing Information Literacy 71
    Developing Critical Thinking 72
    Strategy 1: Writing/Keeping a Journal 73
    Strategy 2: Challenging Learners as They Develop Questions
        and Pose Problems 77
    Strategy 3: Tapping Prior Knowledge 81
    Strategy 4: Building Background...83
    Strategy 5: Using Graphic Organizers...84
    Strategy 6: Guiding Students Into, Through, and Beyond
        Learning Resources 90
    Strategy 7: Developing Effective Searches 91
    Strategy 8: I-Search: Personalizing a Research Project/Paper 97
    Strategy 9: Establishing Audience..99
    Strategy 10: Collaborative Grouping/Cooperative Learning 101
    Strategy 11: Tapping the Multiple Intelligences...104
    Strategy 12: Specially Designed Academic Instruction
        in English (SDAIE)..105
    Instructional Planning Checklist 108
    Instructional Planning Matrix 109
    Notes 110

Chapter 7
  Information Literacy in Action: Sample Scenarios..113
    Search Scenarios 114
    1. Owl in Distress 114
    2. How Much Should We Charge? 116
    3. Relating Literature to Life 117
    4. Where Do I Begin? 118
    5. Waste Disposal Plant 122
    6. Brainstorming Resources 124
    7. Picturing History 125
    8. Identifying an Audience and a Reason to Write 126
    9. Sharing Languages and Organizing Data 127
    10. Radio DJs: A Constructivist Internet Lesson 128
    Notes 130

Appendix A: Rubrics for the Assessment of Information Literacy 131

Appendix B: Research Process Competencies: A Planning Guide 143

Index 155

Introduction

This handbook is intended as a useful guide for classroom teachers, library media specialists, and others who wish to integrate information literacy into their curriculum. It provides both models and strategies that encourage children and young adults to find, analyze, create and use information as they become productive citizens.

Chapter 1: Schooling for an Information Society
The explosion of information in the past decade has lead to a growing awareness that the need for information skills is critical and universal. The increasing diversity of our population demands that we acknowledge sources of information in all languages and recognize that students can and must be information literate in the language in which they communicate. Information literacy is inherent in a thinking, meaning-centered curriculum for all students.

Chapter 2: Information Literacy: A Definition
Information literacy is defined in terms of personal outcomes. Characteristics of an information-literate person are identified and an information literacy model is described. These concepts form the framework on which the rest of the document is based. The chapter ends with a summary of past and current emphases describing the shift from library skills to information literacy.

Chapter 3: The Search Process: Searcher Behaviors and Competencies
This chapter expands the central column of the information literacy model described in chapter two. Characteristic searcher behaviors and competencies for each stage of the search process are described.

Chapter 4: Instructional Planning for Information Literacy: A Team Approach
The curricular planning team that collaborates to guide students toward information literacy includes classroom teachers, library media specialists, bilingual/ESL specialists and aides, other specialists, and the students themselves. Characteristics of both traditional and constructivist approaches to instruction are summarized and related planning processes outlined. Sample curriculum-based problems/units are described in both traditional and constructivist approaches. A checklist on assessing teaching and learning concludes the chapter.

Chapter 5: The Instructional Process: Resource-Based Learning
Resource-based learning requires the planning team to be facilitators who structure the learning environment and guide, track, and assess student learning. The resources on which such learning is based are found in the home, school, community, and beyond, and include people, places, print, and technology.

Chapter 6: The Instructional Process: Strategies for Developing Information Literacy
Instructional strategies for information literacy are presented for various subjects and grade levels. The purpose of each is to engage learners in some aspect of the information literacy model in a way that they might build skill and reflect upon the process. Strategies for English/second language learners are also provided.

Chapter 7: Information Literacy in Action: Sample Scenarios
Various scenarios are offered as examples of searchers at all levels meaningfully engaged in the search process. Although these are not intended as lesson plans, potential implications for curricula are obvious. Taken from real life, most scenarios are interdisciplinary.

Appendix A: Rubrics for the Assessment of Information Literacy
The Colorado Department of Education has developed an instrument that will help students and teachers define and assess levels of competence in the component skills of information literacy.

Appendix B: Research Process Competencies: A Planning Guide
The list of research process competencies introduced in Chapter three is redesigned as a planning guide that may be reproduced. It is intended to assist in curriculum development and to facilitate collaboration between classroom teachers and library media specialists.

Chapter 1

Schooling for an Information Society

In the Information world each student:
1. Constructs meaning,
2. Explores beyond basic curricular content,
3. Self-regulates learning,
4. Makes connections to existing knowledge, and
5. Functions well in a learning environment.

Information in Today's World

Information Literacy has been defined as "the ability to access, evaluate, and use information from a variety of sources."[1] In the physical world how well you use a stick, a shovel, or a back hoe will determine how fast or efficiently you can dig a hole. How you organize your business as a building contractor will determine how many houses you can build in a year. Will each home be designed separately from start to finish or will several basic designs be used repeatedly with minor modifications?

In the information world, every person must have the tools needed to deal with the information age. We know that the types of tools people learn to use will help them cope either efficiently or inefficiently with a world of information that is growing so fast and so complex that it may become overwhelming to even the best of minds.

Information Literacy? What Is All the Fuss?

Once upon a time, that is, in the youth of all adult readers of this publication, we took the mastery of information for granted. We assumed that all the information we needed was in libraries, that librarians knew all the answers, and that learning a few basic reference skills would allow us to unlock most of the information ourselves.

Over the past few years, we have begun to realize that this view is anachronistic. In fact, we know now that our previous mode was not even appropriate for that past in which information seemed finite. Information is more than printed words on the pages of books. It is even more than the tons of data that flow in torrential volume through telephone wires, and more than the tornadoes of voice, data, and images that swirl through the air waves. Information is the stuff of our lives. Information is not just born in ivory towers or decreed by anointed authorities. It is not only what we digest; it is also that which we create.

> Since 1945, the global economic core has shifted from industry and manufacturing to technology and service. Not mineral and metals, but knowledge and information are the new economy's strategic resources. This dramatic change means that, increasingly, employers will expect their workers to be better thinkers and problem solvers. Even the most routine and simple jobs will require higher-order thinking skills. Workers will be expected to think abstractly, critically, and creatively; to organize information; and to work cooperatively with others.[2]

Information literacy strikes a chord of understanding. It seems to connote the ability to master information in the way that literacy suggests mastering text. In a world overwhelmed by information, information literacy is essential.

Language, Culture, and Information: What Are the Connections?

Language allows us to communicate and is essential to all elements of information literacy. We use language to access, to evaluate, and to use information effectively. However, the concept of information is not unique or specific to any language. People in all countries of the world acquire information about their environment, community, and history — all aspects of their culture — and share this information with each other in many ways and in many languages.

Because information can be communicated in any language, information literacy can be developed in any of the more than 100 languages spoken by students in our schools. All learners should be able to access information in any language they know, evaluate it in a language with which they are most comfortable, and then use the information in the language that is most appropriate for their purpose. It is the basic premise of this document that students can and must develop information literacy in any of the languages in which they access, evaluate, and use information.

Language does not exist as a separate entity. Each language is a product of its culture, and the language we use affects our processing of information. Elizabeth Hartung Cole, a bilingual coordinator in the Long Beach Unified School District in Long Beach, California, shares an anecdote from her own experiences that gave her new insights into language and meaning across cultures.

> ▼ Once, during a literature unit, a class, comprised of native and non-native English-speaking students was working on a clustering activity. The center word was white. Native English speakers were contributing words such as clean and snow. Then one student's voice confidently stated, death. Surprised silence filled the room until the student explained that death was commonly associated with the color white in her native country and gave the cultural reasons for it. This helped the class become aware of the intertwined relationship of language and culture and they discussed the possible inaccuracies they might find in reading and analyzing a translated literary work. Fortunately for all, that student felt the class was a culturally and linguistically safe environment, one in which her contribution would be perceived as an enrichment rather than a detraction or wrong answer.[3]

In a recent article titled "The Wonders of Diversity in Our Classrooms," Gail Marshall reminds us that differences in ways of thinking and problem solving add strength when we accommodate and incorporate them as part of the rich cultural of our classrooms:

Chapter 1 • Schooling for an Information Society

▼ Ways of thinking and knowing are not fixed and universal. Instead, they're affected by the environment and by the different and sometimes separate ways cultures solve problems large and small. So we should expect students from different cultures to respond differently to a wide range of tasks. When a student enters our classroom and that student comes from a culture that is different from our own, we should ask, "Now what does this student know about knowing that is different from and more interesting/more productive/more direct/more robust than the ways we're used to working?"[4]

When we speak of developing information literacy, everyone – student, teacher, librarian – is a learner. We become better facilitators of learning when we consider and analyze our own personal paths to learning. How do we get information in real life? Whom do we ask? Where do we look? When do we go to the phone book? When do we go to the library? If we move to another neighborhood or another state, how do we get information? How do we evaluate and use the information we have located? Most important, when and how did we acquire the knowledge and understanding that lets us know the answers to these questions? How did we become information literate?

If we were in a country in which the language was unfamiliar to us, what information needs might we have and how could we meet them? How would we feel if our daily sources of information were available only in a language we did not know? How might we react if the school and public libraries in that country did not provide us with resources in our language? What other sources of information might we explore? How would we change our ways of seeking and obtaining information? What frustrations would we face and how could we lessen those? Careful analysis of these questions can help us to become more empathetic as we consider the information needs of our students who are English learners.

How can we share our insights with students so that they can apply them to their own learning? And what insights about their own worlds of information can students bring to their own personal learning and to the learning communities of their classrooms, neighborhoods, and families? What skills have they already developed in their primary language that will be brought into their learning in English? These are important questions that we will address in our effort to help students to become information literate in any language.

A Thinking, Meaning-Centered Curriculum

The California Department of Education has identified the "thinking-meaning-centered curriculum" as the core of a quality educational program. The following description makes it clear that the goals of such a program include information literacy for all:

If the United States is to compete successfully in the new global market, curriculum must be adjusted to reflect the demands of the knowledge-work economy. The thinking, meaning-centered curriculum incorporates the needed adjustments and has the fundamental goal of enabling students to become independent thinkers, discoverers, and inventors. It is a curriculum for all students, not just the educational elite. Five major themes pervade the thinking, meaning-centered curriculum:

1. Construction of Meaning
   - Students need to become active learners constructing their own knowledge.
   - Students need meaningful interactions.
   - Students need tools to research, inquire, discover, and invent knowledge.
   - Teachers need to shift from conveyers of knowledge to facilitators of learning.

2. Elaboration Beyond Content
   - Students need to build upon new knowledge.
   - Students need to adapt information to new situations.
   - Students need to make inferences, research ideas, and experiment.
   - Students need to use their skills of thinking and problem solving.

3. Self-Regulation of Learning
   - Students need to learn how to learn.
   - Students need to manage, monitor, and evaluate their own learning.
   - Students need to consider a variety of approaches and select the most efficient methods.

4. Connections to Existing Knowledge
   - Students need to make sense of new information by connecting it to what they already know.
   - Students need concrete examples and experiences to deepen understanding.
   - Students need to evaluate new information in reference to what is known.

5. Interaction Within a Personally Meaningful Learning Environment
   - Students need to deal with real situations, problems, and experiences.
   - Students need a learning environment that encourages perseverance, time to work things out, and the acceptance of mistakes as building blocks.[5]

Information Literacy for All

National reform documents, state curriculum frameworks or guidelines, program quality review documents, task force reports, and the national and state publications on information literacy support the idea that the thinking, meaning-centered curriculum is essential for all students and that all students must be lifelong learners.[6]

Information literacy, too, must be for all students whether they are the best and the brightest, the disadvantaged, the English learner or the student with a severe disability. This handbook emphasizes the strategies, techniques and scenarios that take into consideration the common needs of all students to become information literate. In addition, this text includes the strategies, techniques and scenarios that are unique to the several million students in this country whose primary language is other than English.

NOTES

1. Doyle, Christina, *Final Report to the National Forum on Information Literacy*, 1992.
2. *Program Quality Review Training Materials for Elementary and Middle Level Schools*, California Department of Education, 1994, p. 59.
3. Personal interview with Elizabeth Hartung Cole.
4. Gail Marshall, "The Wonders of Diversity in Our Classrooms," *CUE Newsletter*, January/February, 1995, p. 1-3.
5. *Program Quality Review Training Materials for Elementary and Middle Level Schools*, California Department of Education, 1994, p. 71.
6. One of the most recent calls to action is: U.S. Department of Education, *Building Knowledge for a Nation of Learners: A Framework for Education Research 1997*, A Report by the Assistant Secretary, Office of Educational Research and Improvement, Sharon P. Robinson, and the National Educational Research Policy and Priorities Board, December, 1996. (ISBN 0-16-048944-X)

Chapter 2

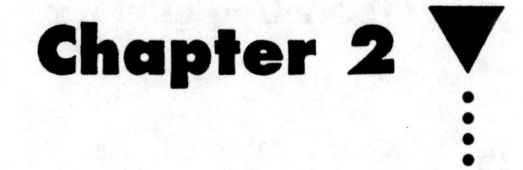

Information Literacy: A Definition

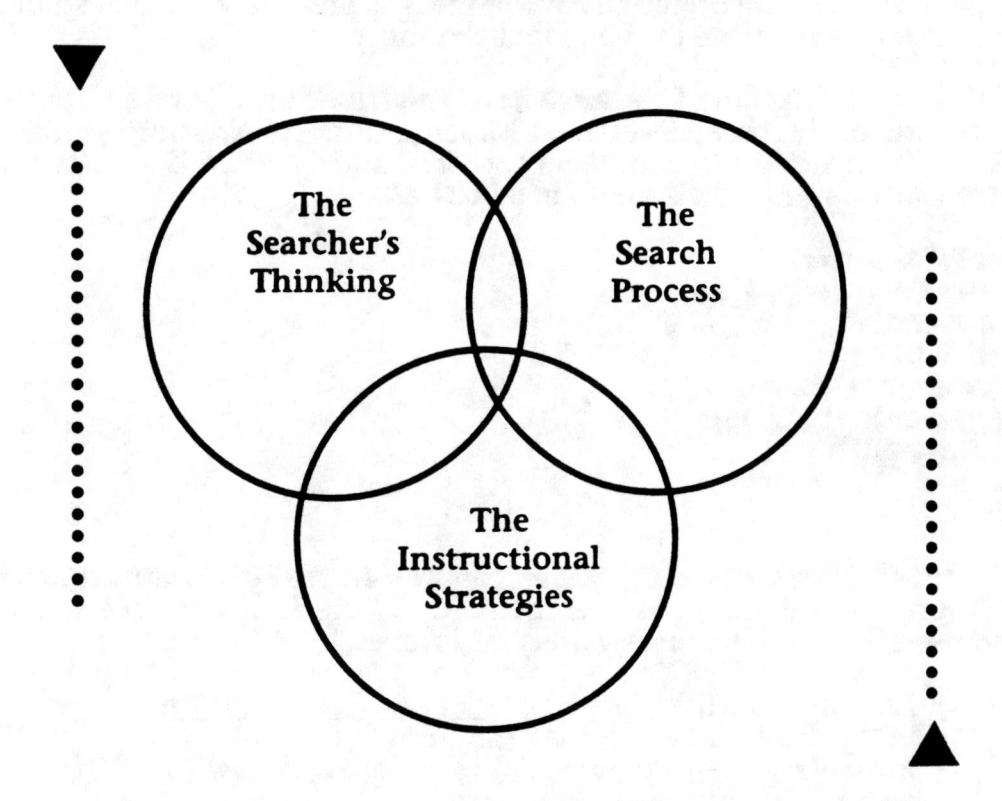

- The Searcher's Thinking
- The Search Process
- The Instructional Strategies

Information Literacy

Rationale

Information literacy has become a catch phrase. Its popularity reflects a growing awareness that what we have generally encompassed by the term "literacy" has somehow omitted the consideration of how or why we use the tools of literacy to find the information that answers our questions or satisfies our curiosity. It is easy to define literacy as a person reading, but we also must reflect on how the reader might evaluate and use the information that is read.

Our awareness of the need for information literacy is related to our recognition that survival skills are important to all people and are independent of any specific language. And if information literacy is valuable in one language, then information literacy in two languages provides bilingual students with an obvious advantage in the global economy.

The following description of the citizens of the 21st century is a synthesis of reform reports of the past 15 years. *A Nation at Risk*, *A Nation Prepared*, the SCANS report on *What Work Requires of Schools*, and *Goals 2000* all agree that the citizens of the 21st century will need to be:

- Problem solvers,
- Effective questioners,
- Cooperative workers,
- Self-starters,
- Information managers,
- Flexible thinkers, and
- Multilingual[1]

Definition

To attain these skills, citizens of the 21st century must also be information literate. Information literacy has been defined as "the ability to access, evaluate, and use information from a variety of sources."[2]

- An information-literate person **accesses information**.
    - Recognizes the need for information.
    - Recognizes that accurate and complete information is the basis for intelligent decision making.
    - Formulates questions based on the need for information.
    - Identifies potential sources of information.
    - Develops successful search strategies.
    - Accesses print and technology-based sources of information.

- An information-literate person **evaluates information**.
    - Establishes authority.
    - Determines accuracy and relevance.
    - Recognizes point of view and perspective.

- An information-literate person **uses information**.
    - Organizes information for practical application.

- Integrates new information into an existing body of knowledge.
- Uses information in critical thinking and problem solving.

An Information Literacy Model

Although the definition of information literacy may appear to be simple, the concept is complex. Recent research regarding the nature of information literacy has resulted in the development of several search process models. The model that emerges on the following pages is a synthesis of existing models. It is reproduced here as the basis for the discussion of integrating information literacy into all areas of the curriculum for all students in all languages.

The model can be viewed from three different perspectives as shown in Figure 1:
- The searcher's thinking,
- The search process, and
- The instructional strategies.

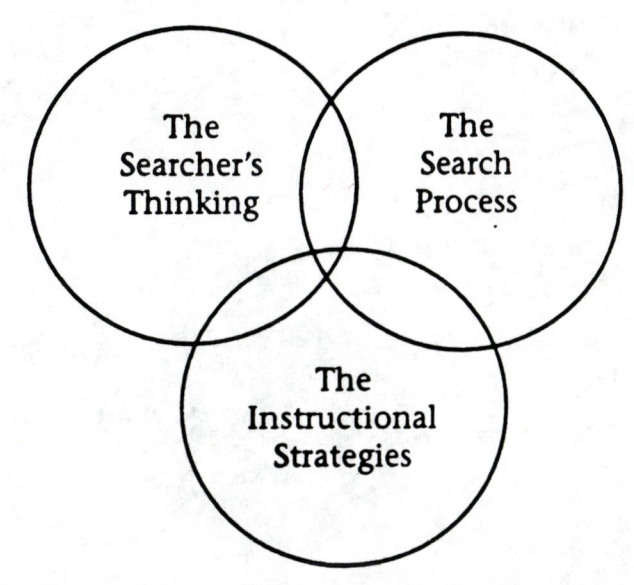

Figure 1: An Information Literacy Model - Three Interdependent Processes

Each of the components in the model is interdependent; that is, the thinking process stimulates the search process, which in turn determines an appropriate instructional strategy. The resulting model is not linear, but one that flows, branches, and loops in different ways for each searcher and each search.

▼ Chapter 2 • Information Literacy

The Searcher's Thinking

The first component of the information literacy model considers what a person might be thinking when confronting an information problem. A searcher's thinking pattern might look something like the following diagram:

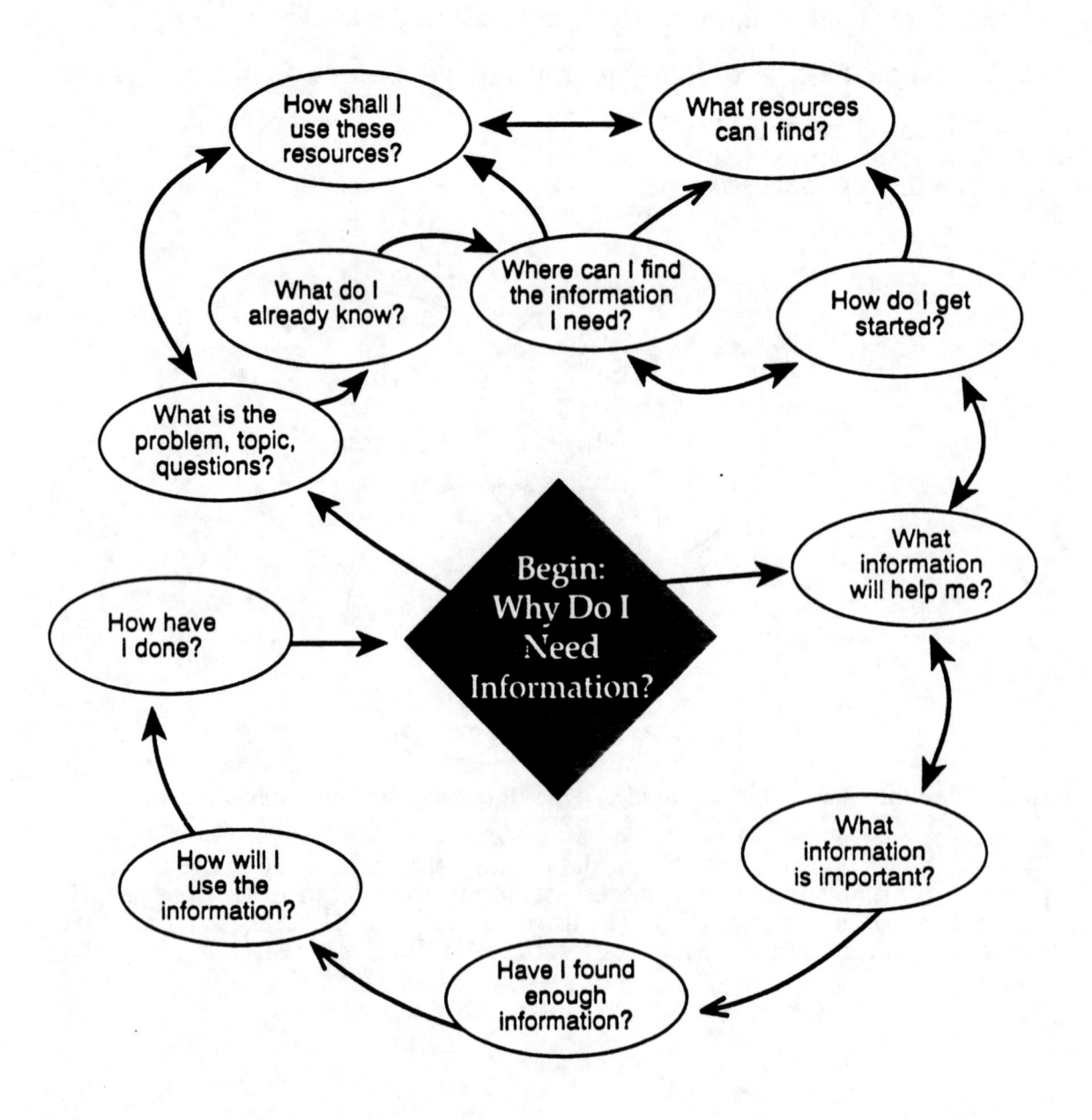

Figure 2: The Searcher's Thinking

The Search Process

The second component of the information literacy model describes the search process. It suggests a systematic way of approaching an information problem. While specific stages can be identified, the search process will look different for each person and for each problem. The process might look something like the following diagram:

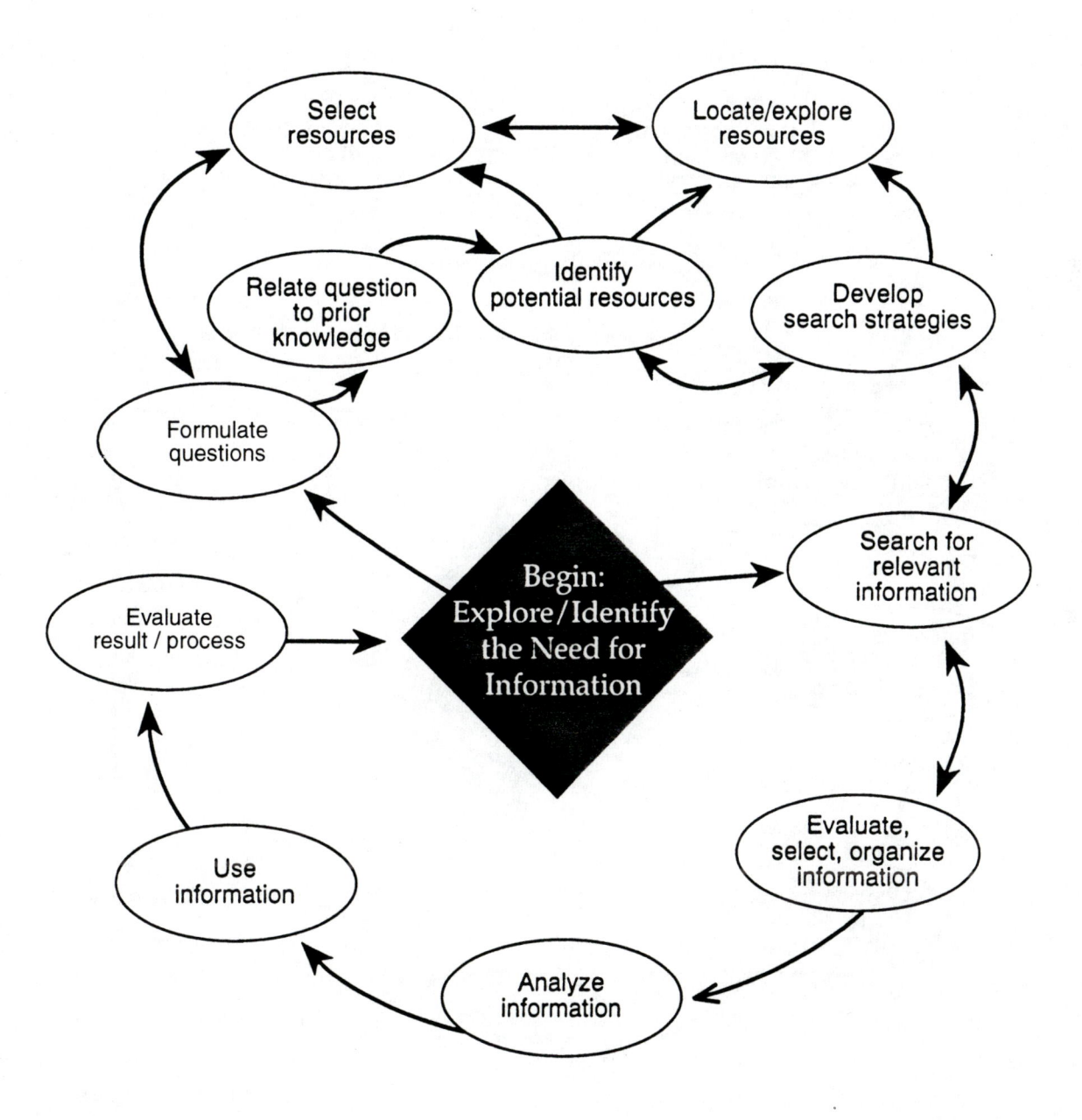

Figure 3: The Search Process

The Instructional Strategies

The third component of the information literacy model consists of the instructional strategies that might be generated in response to the learner's needs during the search process. The teacher introduces/suggests a particular strategy to meet a particular need rather than attempting to impose a fixed set of strategies on all searchers. Patterns of instructional support will vary depending on the searcher, the problem, and the resources.

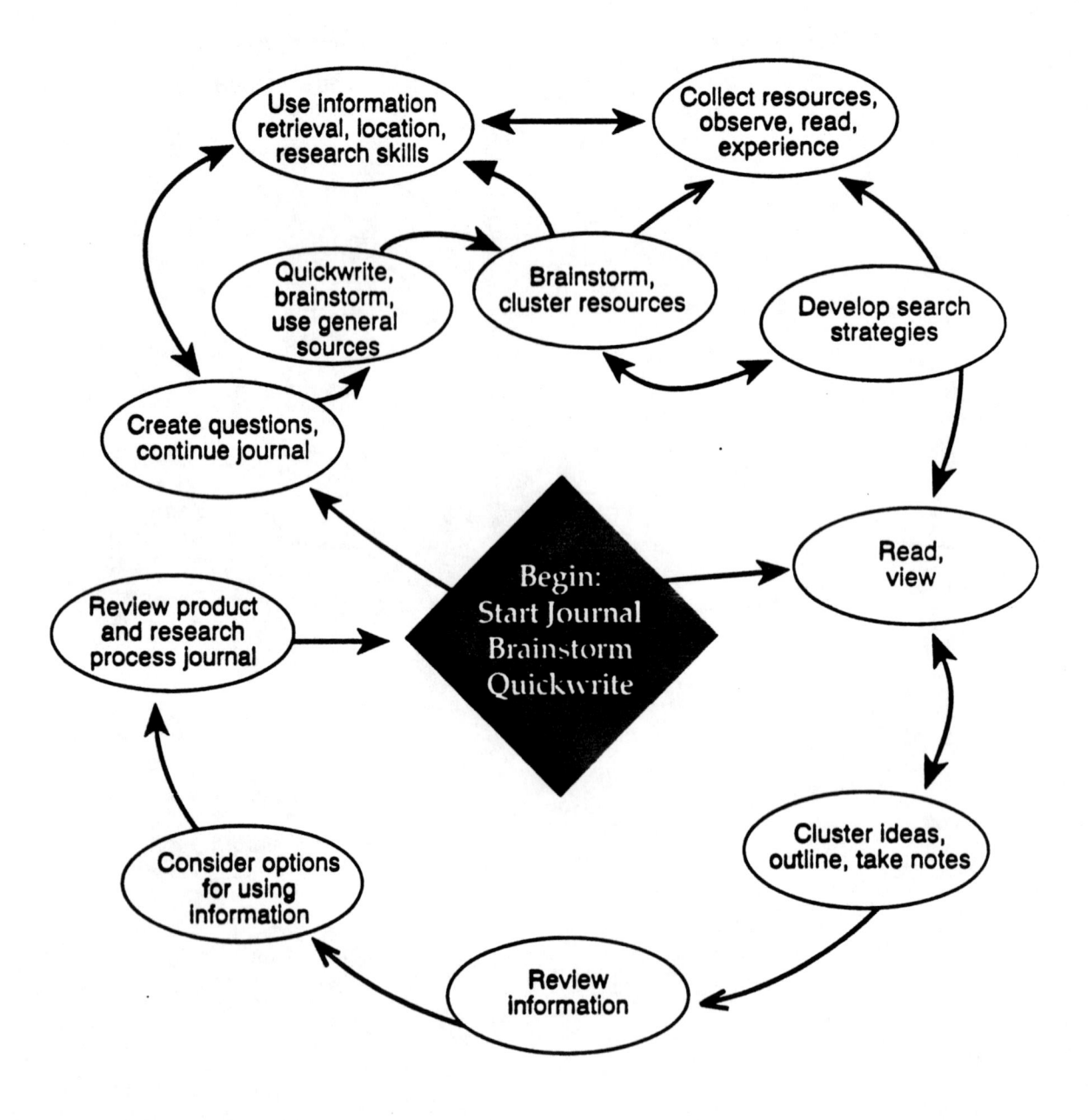

Figure 4: The Instructional Strategies

The Information Literacy Model Summary[3]

The searcher's thinking, the search process, and instructional strategies are brought together in this information literacy model. While the presentation below is linear, the process and the interaction of the components are not. However, the linear presentation shows how a searcher's thinking can trigger a stage in the search process, which in turn suggests a supportive instructional strategy. For example, "Why do I need information?" may trigger the search process stage of "Exploring the need for information" which in turn triggers the instructional strategy of "Beginning a journal to track the search process."

Searcher's Thinking	Search Process	Instructional Strategies
Why do I need information?	Explore/identify the need for information.	Begin journal to track the search process. Brainstorm/cluster/discuss/map. Quickwrite.
What is the problem, topic or question?	Formulate the central search question.	Create possible questions. Continue journal at each step.
What do I already know about this problem/topic/question? What must I find out?	Relate the question to prior knowledge. Identify key words, concepts, and names.	Quickwrite. Brainstorm/cluster/map. Use general information sources for background.
Where can I find the information I need? Are there people I can ask? Is the information in my classroom or library media center? Are there resources in my community?	Identify potential resources. How accessible is each?	Brainstorm possible resources. Cluster resources by type, location, etc. Create checklist of resources: How appropriate is each?
How do I get started? What are some key words/topics/ideas? Where do I go first?	Develop general strategies to organize the search.	Develop key word and Boolean search strategies.
What resources can I find? Which can I use?	Locate and explore previously identified resources.	Interview people. Go to libraries, museums, information centers. Collect resources. Observe/experience/read.

▼ Chapter 2 • Information Literacy

How shall I use/search these resources? How will I find the Information I need? What strategies should I use?	Select the most useful resources for further exploration and formulate specific strategies for using them.	Develop search strategies. Use information retrieval/location/ research skills.
What information will help me?	Search for relevant information in these resources.	Read and view.
What should I record? What is important? How could I record it? How could I arrange it?	Evaluate, select, and organize information.	Cluster ideas into subtopics. Use outlining and notetaking skills.
Have I found the information I need? Should I look further?	Analyze information retrieved; determine its relevance; interpret, infer, and synthesize.	Review information to see if it meets original needs.
How will I use/present the information? Who is my audience? In what form could I use/present it? How can I structure it?	Determine how to use/ present/communicate information. Organize information for intended use.	Consider options for presenting information. Make needed decisions. Solve original problems. Develop written, visual, oral, multimedia or other presentation.
How have I done? ...in my opinion? ...according to others? What knowledge have I gained? What skills have I learned? What could I improve and how?	Use information. Evaluate results. Evaluate process.	Review the product. Review the search process journal. Review with teacher, family, peers. Plan changes for next project.

14

Information Literacy

From Library Skills to Information Literacy: New Approaches

Through the progression on the previous pages, an information literacy model emerges. How is this model different from a continuum of library skills? How is information literacy different from previous approaches? The differences are best understood as changes of emphasis. The chart below compares past and current emphases.

Past Emphasis	Current Emphasis
Teacher-identified research topics or projects	Student collaboration in identifying relevant issues to consider
Locating information	Evaluating and using/applying information
Activities/information/resources available in English	Activities/information/resources available in many languages
Printed material	All sources of information (e.g., people, technology, artifacts, print)
Secondary sources	Primary sources
Established authority of reference sources	Questioning and identifying point of view
Single perspective	Multiple perspectives
Product, usually a paper	Thinking and problem-solving of the search process and the application of information
Presenting results in written or oral language always in English	Presenting results in a variety of formats and in many languages

The current emphasis, with its focus on the searcher, acknowledges and makes constructive use of the rich diversity of learners, learning styles, languages, and resources in our multicultural, multilingual society.

Developing Your Own Information Literacy Model

The information literacy model recommended in this publication is just that - a recommended model. If a program of information literacy is to succeed in a school, then an information literacy model must be "owned" by the library media specialist and the teachers in that building. This means that educators need to develop their own mental model from which a school-wide plan for information literacy will emerge.

Building a commonly-shared vision of information literacy takes time. This could be done in a day-long inservice or a retreat where all the interested players consider the topic. One tested method is to brief a group on a definition of information literacy and then let them make comparisons with a number of information literacy models. They are then asked to consider what the students in their own school need and are asked to synthesize a model that they can all support. In other words, in a day-long activity, they use one information literacy model to produce a new model that will work for them. In a reflection of the day's work, the group could compare their own difficulties and experiences with what students will be doing as they begin to use the information literacy model.

If the faculty of the school has come to consensus on an information literacy model, then they will start to integrate information literacy concepts into their work as a natural part of the teaching process. For each person, an individualized and internalized model is an icon that helps to think about a new way to process information. Teachers begin to realize that the information literacy model is something revised and adapted as new problems are confronted in the teaching and learning process.

The following list of models is drawn from the field of school libraries and a few from other disciplines. Other models should be sought to add richness to the discussion.

Information Literacy Models From the School Library Media Field

American Association of School Librarians, "Information Literacy Standards for Student Learning," *AASL Hotline/Connections*, Fall, 1996, p. 2-3. (note: these standards are in draft form. Final publication of the standards is scheduled for 1998).

Colorado Department of Education and Colorado Educational Media Association, *Model Information Literacy Guidelines*, 1994. See also by the same associations *Rubrics for the Assessment of Information Literacy*, 1996 (in Appendix A).

California School Library Association, *From Library Skills to Information Literacy: A Handbook for the 21st Century*, 2nd ed., Castle Rock, CO: Hi Willow Research & Publishing, 1997.

Kuhlthau, Carol Collier, *Seeking Meaning: A Process Approach to Library and Information Services*, Norwood, NJ: Ablex, 1993.

Eisenberg, Michael B. And Robert E. Berkowitz, *Information Problem Solving: The Big Six Skills Approach to Library & Information Skills Instruction*, Norwood, NJ: Ablex, 1990.

Stripling, Barbara K. and Judy M. Pitts, *Brainstorms and Blueprints: Teaching Library Research as a Thinking Process*, Englewood, CO: Libraries Unlimited, 1988.

Loertscher, David V., "All That Glitters May Not Be Gold," *Emergency Librarian*, November-December, 1996, p. 21-25.

Pappas, Marjorie, "Information Skills Model," in: *Teaching Electronic Information Skills*, The Follett Software Company, 1995. (three binders as follows: Grades K-5; Grades 6-8; Grades 9-12; approx. $75 each). 1391 Corporate Drive, McHenry, IL 60050-7041.

Samples From Other Disciplines

Architecture
Von Wodtke, Mark, *Mind Over Media: Creative Thinking Skills for Electronic Media*, New York: McGraw-Hill, 1993.

History
"Standards in Historical Thinking" printed in each volume of the National Standards for History, National Center for History in the Schools, University of California, Los Angeles, 1994. (10880 Wilshire Blvd., Suite 761, Los Angeles, CA 90024-4108) Example: *National Standards for History for Grades K-4: Expanding Children's World in Time and Space*, p. 15-27.

Language Arts
"IRA/NCTE Standards for the English Language Arts," *Standards for the English Language Arts*, International Reading Association and National Council of Teachers of English, 1996, p. 3. (International Reading Association 800 Barksdale Road, P.O. Box 8139, Newark, Delaware 19714-8139)

NOTES

1. The list of characteristics is taken from: Program *Quality Review Training Materials for Elementary and Middle Level Schools*, California Department of Education, 1994, p. 19.
2. Both the definition of information literacy and the characteristics of an information-literate person are derived from the research of Dr. Christine S. Doyle as reported in her monograph: *Information Literacy in an Information Society: A Concept for the Information Age*, ERIC Clearinghouse on Information and Technology, June, 1994.
3. The entire information literacy model has been adapted and expanded from *Research as a Process: Developing Skills for Life in an Information Society*, Los Angeles County Office of Education, 1989.

Chapter 3 ▼

The Search Process
Searcher Behaviors and Competencies

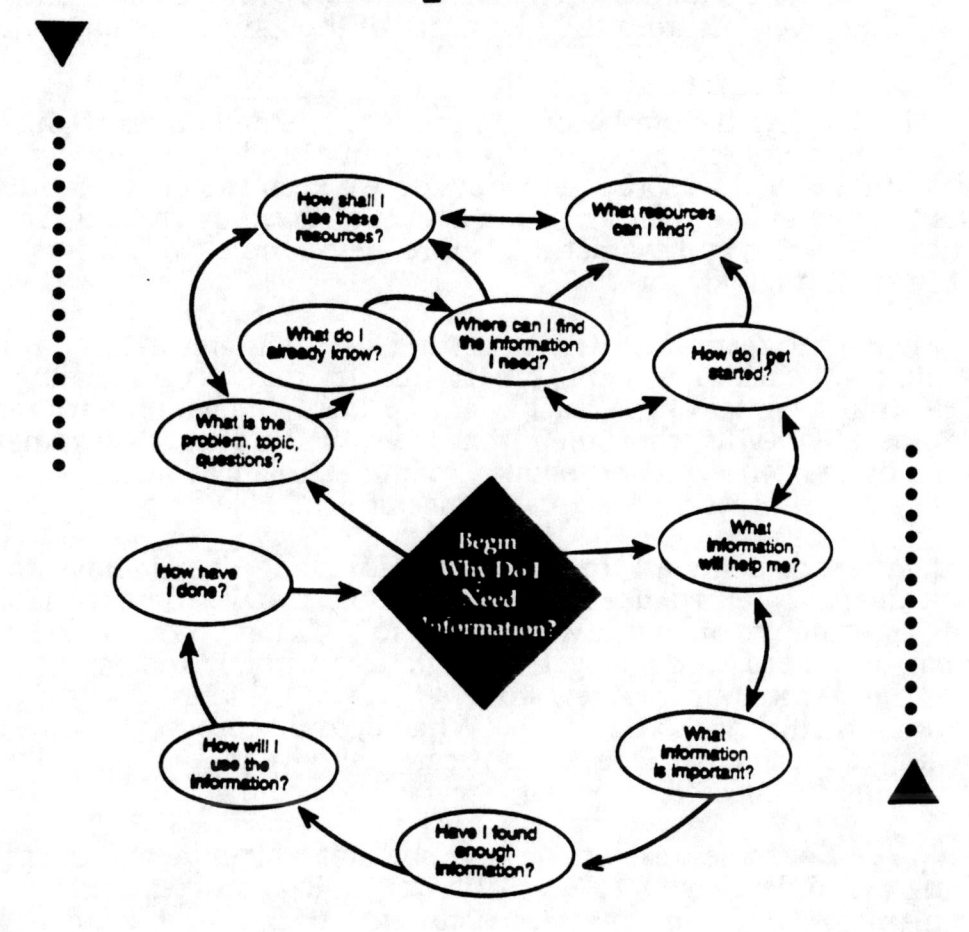

(Diagram: a cyclical flowchart centered on a black diamond labeled "Begin Why Do I Need Information?" surrounded by ovals containing the questions: "How shall I use these resources?", "What resources can I find?", "What do I already know?", "Where can I find the information I need?", "How do I get started?", "What is the problem, topic, questions?", "What information will help me?", "How have I done?", "How will I use the information?", "What information is important?", "Have I found enough information?")

The Search Process

On Waiting for Real Life to Begin

What is research? Is it looking things up, gathering facts, checking encyclopedias and almanacs, roaming the Internet? How do we keep research from becoming so product oriented that the process itself is lost? And when does the product assume more importance than the process? At some point it must, mustn't it?

The result of research is a product, but research itself is the process of 'looking for' and 'looking for' again. *The Random House Dictionary* lists 14 meanings for the word *search;* they all involve activity. *Process* is defined as a systematic series of actions directed toward some end. In recent years we have learned about the writing process, the reading process, and even the literature process. Frank Smith talks about the literacy club as the natural method of learning to read as we learn to speak.[1] The search process reflects the way most of us instinctively set about solving problems from the first flurry of thought to the ultimate resolution.

How do we keep research from becoming product oriented rather than process oriented? At some point, of course, it must result in a product: an answer, a solution, a diagram, or even a report. But how do we keep students from rushing toward the product before their attention is ever engaged by the satisfaction of investigation, discovery, and evaluation: before they complete the process which will result in fresh original work?

Students I see want to roam the Internet, getting lost on interesting byways, hoping something will click. For many, it's try this, try that, get something down on paper. Fulfill the letter of the teacher's assignment and get on with real life. The process usually begins when the teacher tells the student to do something: prepare for a debate, write a report about a mammal, role play an important figure in history, make a speech, design a science project...

The first question students ask (other than "How long does it have to be?", "When is it due?", "Can we use a pencil?", "Does it have to be in handwriting?", and "How many points is it worth?") is not, "What do I need to know?", but, "What do I need to do to get through this without too much pain?"; "What does the teacher want?" A few students get really interested and dig deep; the rest lean on their shovels and watch. When does this process become something students can really use? Does anyone care? Or have they all drifted off into la-la land waiting for the bell to ring and real life to begin again?

The search process becomes real when the problem is real and when the product is something the student, age 8 to 80, really wants. Real problems are: the job I want; the man/woman I want to marry; a cure for AIDS, cancer, acne, or heartbreak; being too tall/ too short; being childless; buying a house or renting an apartment; finding a plumber, a hairdresser, or a doctor. Sometimes the answers are as simple as asking a good friend or looking in the telephone directory, but often the course of the search is difficult, complex, and just the beginning of a longer search.

Can we help students simulate this feeling now — this urge to seek, to plunge in, to find out, to ask questions? One possibility is to develop the model of the search process and apply it to our own classroom scenarios.

The model that follows has been designed for that purpose. We need to apply it tightly so that every teacher activity is yanked out and every student activity strengthened; we need to make it child-centered and directed; we need to worry less about whether it's something we can put up at Open House and more about whether it's a vehicle for learning the process of active involved thought. The real life that students are so eager to get back to has its true beginning when it becomes merged with what happens in the classroom. It begins when students perceive that the process they use to solve class-generated problems can be the same one they use to meet the challenges of being a human in an increasingly complex world.[2]

The Search Process: Searcher Behaviors and Competencies

The search process begins when an individual first identifies a need for information, then continues by going through stages to access, evaluate, and use the information. The search process is synthesized as information literacy when the searcher finally analyzes and evaluates the results of the process and internalizes it for future application.

Each stage of the search process can be further amplified by a description of behaviors and competencies suggested as responses to the searchers' questions. Those developed below are only some of the possible responses and understandings inherent in the search process. Classroom teachers, library media specialists, bilingual/ESL specialists, and students will discover a myriad of others as they analyze how learners approach and progress through the search process. Note that the headings below refer to the Search Process Stages of the Information Literacy Model.

EXPLORE/IDENTIFY THE NEED FOR INFORMATION.

In life outside school, the quest for information usually begins as a response to a need or an interest. Students need guided experiences in defining their personal needs for information.

In school, the need for information is often in the form of an assignment or an engaging problem. If so, the students need to know what the parameters of the assignment are, and how the search process and any product will be evaluated. They also need to be able to choose questions or topics of personal interest.

Searchers will...
    A. Identify the assignment or other purpose for which information is needed.
    B. Identify general types of questions or other information needs.
    C. Begin a search process log/journal.
        1. Generate ideas using individual and group brainstorming strategies, e.g., discussion, quickwrite.
        2. Use cluster and map techniques to organize brainstorming notations.

FORMULATE THE CENTRAL SEARCH QUESTION.

Whatever the impetus for seeking and using information, there is an advantage to formulating a central question as the first step of the quest. Thinking in terms of a research question rather than a "topic" provides focus for the search.

Information Literacy

Searchers will...
- A. Use a variety of questioning strategies (yes/no, open-ended, probing) to create possible questions related to the identified need for information.
- B. Focus the purpose of the search by formulating a specific question to be answered.
- C. Develop a preliminary central question or thesis statement.

RELATE QUESTION TO PREVIOUS KNOWLEDGE; IDENTIFY KEY WORDS, CONCEPTS, AND NAMES.

If information is to have meaning, students must make connections between new information and previous experiences or knowledge. Lack of understanding may result in frustration, plagiarism, and incoherence. The first step in orienting oneself to an unfamiliar subject is to find one or more existing connections that give the subject meaning.

The process begins with thoughtful consideration of what is already known that is related and useful. Students begin to make note of key words, concepts, and names related to the search question. After that, there may be a need to consult general sources and knowledgeable people to add to the list of key words and concepts. It is important to distinguish this step from the beginning of the search itself so that attention is focused on relationships and key terms, rather than on factual detail.

Searchers will...
- A. Record previous knowledge relating to the central question.
    1. Quickwrite.
    2. Brainstorm ideas and information about the central question by recalling previous experiences.
    3. Note key words, concepts, and names related to the search question.
    4. Demonstrate the ability to use a variety of strategies to organize known information: list, cluster, traditional outline, mind map, radial outline.
- B. Review the search process journal to determine missing elements.
- C. When previous knowledge is limited, use general sources of information (e.g., a knowledgeable person, encyclopedias) to focus on relationships and key terms for overview of topic.
    1. Skim encyclopedia articles, chapters in books, web sites, outlines, or summaries on the topic.
    2. Use video or other technology resources that present general overviews of the topic.
    3. Interview a knowledgeable person.
- D. Restate phrases/concepts in their own words.

IDENTIFY POTENTIAL RESOURCES.

Everyone has had experiences with a broad range of resources that are of potential use in exploring information or solving problems. After students relate the search question to their previous knowledge, they must begin to identify general and specific resources relevant to the question. This involves more brainstorming and clustering as they list and group resources by type and location.

To be successful in a search for information, searchers must know generally where information comes from and how it is organized in the area of knowledge being searched. It is important that they be aware of the sources that are available—their extent, their quality, and the divergence or convergence of points of view they represent.

The students' understanding of what is available governs the search. Library media specialists and classroom teachers can expand students' awareness and facilitate access to a broad range of resources. These might include: personal interviews, firsthand observations, online searches, web sites, video and laserdisc programs, and print or online subject-specific reference sources.

Searchers will...
    A. Identify potential resources.
        1. List types of resources for seeking desired information, e.g., experts in the field of the search, newspapers, magazines, books, maps, web sites, online databases, audio, and visual resources.
        2. Identify specific resources in each category that may be relevant to the search.
    B. Identify availability of resources and group by location.
    C. Use broad, general resources if more basic information about the search subject is needed.
        1. Use information from dictionaries, encyclopedias, and other general resources to identify major/significant sources of information regarding the central question.
        2. Recall words, terms, methods, facts, concepts, or specific items, by using broad, general information resources.

DEVELOP GENERAL SEARCH STRATEGIES TO ORGANIZE THE SEARCH.

To answer the central question of the search, it is necessary to determine the components of that question and phrase these in subquestions. These subquestions constitute a plan for the search and become tests of relevance for what is found. The basis for formulating these questions is knowledge gained from previous experiences and from the development of key words, lists, and concept outlines. Lists and outlines developed in previous stages can serve as conceptual organizers to help the searcher categorize information and clarify relationships among the terms and ideas.

Searchers will...
    A. Use previously compiled terms and add subject headings and database descriptors that relate to the central question or thesis.
    B. Summarize in simple sentence form the main ideas regarding the central question.
    C. Ask further questions to clarify meaning.
    D. Construct subquestions about the central question.
    E. Discriminate between more important and less important questions and exclude the least important questions.
    F. Create a plan for the search based on the resulting questions.
    G. Organize key words, phrases, and subject headings into Boolean and other relevant search strategies.
    H. Re-analyze search strategies as success or failure is experienced.

LOCATE AND EXPLORE PREVIOUSLY IDENTIFIED RESOURCES.

There are two steps to the basic process of locating and exploring information resources:

1. Locating a citation or reference to a source, and
2. Gaining access to the source itself.

Students learn to use initial sources as a lead to other sources, e.g., using in-source bibliographies, noting the subject headings listed, locating other sources recommended by others. As searchers develop experience in this process, they become more sophisticated in pursuing multiple leads to extend the scope of the information resources they explore.

Searchers will...
A. Locate available resources from those previously identified.
   1. Recognize and use library media center resources, including the consulting role of the library media specialist.
   2. Reconsider general resource materials previously identified, such as periodicals, newspapers, special encyclopedias, electronic sources mentioned earlier.
   3. Consider resources outside the school, e.g., other libraries, museums, community resources, experts, and online resources.
B. Use information access skills.
   1. Recognize that most information sources are indexed and that indexes may be in a variety of formats such as card, print, microform, or online.
   2. Recognize that information is arranged and indexed in one or a combination of ways such as by subject, location, alphabetically, chronologically, on a continuum.
   3. Locate the index for each information source and interpret all information in index entries.
   4. Use subject headings and cross references to find additional resources.
   5. Access relevant records in online databases.
      a. Determine the possible databases to be searched.
      b. Design the search strategy, narrowing or expanding the search parameters as needed.
C. Revise or redefine the central question by narrowing or broadening its focus as necessary.

SELECT THE MOST USEFUL RESOURCES FOR FURTHER EXPLORATION AND FORMULATE SPECIFIC STRATEGIES FOR USING THEM.

Evaluate resources explored thus far. Compare and contrast the format, strengths, and weaknesses of various resources, and their distinctive formats. Finding the most useful information in a film, videotape, or other nonprint medium requires a unique set of skills. A first viewing or listening may serve mainly to pinpoint sections that will be of use; subsequent replaying of those sections will permit detailed note taking. Interviewing people, on the other hand, requires a detailed set of questions and a willingness to improvise as the conversation takes unexpected turns.

Searchers will...
A. Select the most useful resources from those available.
   1. Skim the article, media abstract, or text printout to find a word, name, date, phrase, idea, or general overview of the resource.
   2. Scan/search materials in electronic or other nonprint formats.
B. Conduct primary research as needed.
   1. Plan and complete an interview, experiment, or observation.
   2. Plan and conduct a survey/questionnaire.
   3. Write a letter of inquiry.

C. Revise or redefine the central question or statement by narrowing or broadening as necessary.

SEARCH FOR RELEVANT INFORMATION.

Once the most appropriate resources have been selected, the relevant and useful information must be extracted efficiently. The students must be encouraged to skip quickly over any material that does not contribute to answering the questions previously identified.

Searchers will...
- A. Locate the sections of each resource that are useful in answering the search questions.
    1. Use indexes, tables of contents, headings within chapters, and topic sentences of paragraphs.
    2. Use skimming skills to extract information from selected resources.
    3. Find and make effective use of the relevant sections in nonprint media such as videotapes, films, and audiotapes.
- B. Continue to compile and organize information.
- C. Compare information with search questions.
    1. Identify gaps in information collected.
    2. Determine if additional sources are needed.
- D. Compile bibliographic information for each resource.
- E. Review, evaluate, and update the search process log/journal.

EVALUATE, SELECT, AND ORGANIZE INFORMATION.

As the searcher locates potentially useful bits of information, a screening process takes place. First, the information must pass the test of relevance established by the search questions. Next, it is scrutinized in terms of such factors as currency, authority, objectivity, consistency, and potential for being understood. The level of understanding depends on the student's personal learning style and familiarity with the subject. Information that is useful to one student may be of limited value to another working on the same question. As previously discussed, there can be no understanding of information that does not relate to what is already known. As students progress, they gain skills in applying these and other tests of usefulness. Skill in applying each of these tests must be learned and reinforced through experience. Concurrent with interpreting and evaluating information, the students select the most useful parts of the gathered information. By scanning and skimming, the searcher wastes little time with bits of information that are not useful in answering the central question. This is the fine screening of the information that has already been sorted through previous steps.

One reliable test of a searcher's understanding of a piece of information is the ability to paraphrase it accurately. Developing habits of summarizing and paraphrasing in taking notes makes the searcher think about and interpret information at the time it is accessed, not later when context clues are missing.

In emphasizing the essence, rather than the form of notetaking, it is important to teach the skills of organizing or indexing paraphrased notes according to the search questions (or working outline). This makes the final steps of the process much easier. In some cases, drawing diagrams, making audio recordings, or collecting artifacts may serve instead of written notes as important means for preserving information.

Searchers will...
    A. Screen the potential bits of information.
        1. Choose those that contribute to the search question.
        2. Record the chosen information in an organized way.
    B. Evaluate for currency of information.
        1. Identify copyright date.
        2. Identify the actual date, era, or time the ideas were created.
        3. Understand the significance of dated versus current information, or whether dating is significant at all.
    C. Establish authority.
        1. Identify the contributor/producer of the sources being used.
        2. Evaluate the contributor's/producer's work for motive, point of view, bias, scholarship, intended audience, etc.
    D. Distinguish among fact, opinion, and propaganda.
    E. Select information that is most useful in addressing the central question. Eliminate irrelevant information.
    F. Take notes, using one or more of a variety of notetaking strategies such as highlighting, photocopies, electronic note pad, note cards.
    G. Organize notes and ideas and develop an outline or graphic organizer.

ANALYZE INFORMATION RETRIEVED: INTERPRET, INFER, AND INTEGRATE.

Interpretation skills begin, but do not end, with reading. A good reader makes use of context clues, discerns the structure of a piece of writing, draws inferences, and perceives relationships. Such skills are also essential to such diverse activities as reading maps, interpreting tables of statistical data, reading schematics, studying photographs, viewing films or videos, or reading web pages. During any information quest, the searcher must have the interpretation skills required by each format to retrieve the useful pieces of information or else the whole process becomes meaningless. At this stage, the searcher integrates fragments of information into a comprehensible whole to create personal meaning.

Searchers will...
    A. Read, view, or listen to sources, identifying main ideas, opinions, and supporting facts. Inconsistencies are noticed and questioned.
    B. Interpret graphic sources of information: maps, charts, pictures, diagrams, graphs, tables, etc. Inaccuracies are discovered and rejected.
    C. Derive valid inferences from information sources. Substitute new ideas when information is inaccurate.
    D. Summarize and paraphrase important facts and details that support the central question. Compile notes/information according to the outline previously developed. Create new conclusions from facts using different perspectives.
    E. Review compiled information to bring personal meaning and understanding to the original problem, topic, or question.

DETERMINE HOW TO USE/PRESENT/COMMUNICATE INFORMATION: ORGANIZE INFORMATION FOR INTENDED USE; USE INFORMATION.

Information sources are rarely organized in ways that exactly match the searcher's end use of the content, As notes are created, they are classified in a way that meets the searcher's original need. This classification scheme may evolve during the quest and probably will closely approximate the final structure or outline. In some cases, it may be advantageous to create a new structure or outline.

Students benefit from a variety of experiences in applying information; written reports are only one of them. Students need to reach conclusions and to prepare for activities that are the outcomes of their quests for information. Presentation formats can include papers, dramatizations, panel discussions, multimedia presentations, models, demonstrations, or school-wide projects. Each application has its own set of skills required for success. Interpersonal skills may be as important as language skills, and visual skills as important as verbal ones.

Searchers will...
- A. Determine the most effective method of presentation.
    1. Identify and use appropriate media technologies.
    2. Consider presenting thoughts, feelings, and creative ideas through student-produced media such as books, posters, transparencies, slide shows, puppets, audio and video tapes, web pages, hypermedia, newspapers, or electronic resources.
- B. Plan for projects such as dramatizations, debates, writing, multimedia slide shows, videotape presentations, demonstrations, or exhibits.
    1. Decide on a purpose such as to inform, persuade, entertain, etc.
    2. Select an appropriate organizational style.
    3. Determine the main point to be made or arguments to be developed and adapt a working outline.
    4. Use the composition process including prewriting, rough draft, writing/designing/scripting, etc. (Most forms of presentation require some written planning.)
    5. Prepare a bibliography or list of all references used.
- C. Make a clear, well-supported presentation that answers the central question or solves the problem by applying search information.
- D. Draw conclusions based on gathered information.

EVALUATE RESULTS; EVALUATE PROCESS.

Evaluation is an ongoing activity that includes many checkpoints and involves students and teachers as key figures in the assessment process. Students assess their knowledge, attitudes, and feelings about the project. Teachers guide and monitor skills development. Together, students and teachers assess the product and the process.

Strategies for assessment include teacher and student review of logs or journals and all other documents or products including notes, scraps, etc. Evaluation of the product is a consideration of the total process.

Learners develop the ability to recognize the steps or stages in the thinking process and to internalize them for future application. The teacher aids the process of metacognition by involving the learner in a conscious review and analysis of the search process as a part of the ongoing assessment.

Searchers will...
- A. Evaluate the project and the search process.
    1. Reflect on the process as a whole. What came easy? What was difficult? Why were there barriers? Which could be solved with a different approach?

2. Reflect on the information sources that were used. Were they easy to find? What local libraries and agencies responded poorly or well? Why? What changes in library collections, procedures, and assistance would help in the information gathering process.
3. Review the search process log/journal. Does it show progress in conducting information searches? What kinds of improvements in the process would lead to better results?
4. What is the quality of the product created? Does it show careful analysis, thoughtful content, and good technical execution? Is it creative?[3]

NOTES

1. Smith, Frank, *Joining the Literacy Club: Further Essays Into Education*, Portsmouth, NH: Heinemann, 1988.
2. These insightful musings are from the creative pen of Mary Purucker, librarian, Santa Monica High School, California.
3. The stages of the search process in this chapter are adapted and expanded from *Information Skills Curriculum Guide: Process, Scope and Sequence,* Olympia, WA: Office of Superintendent of Public Instruction in conjunction with the Washington Library Media Association Supervisors Subcommittee on Information Skills, 1987.

Chapter 4

Instructional Planning for Information Literacy: A Team Approach

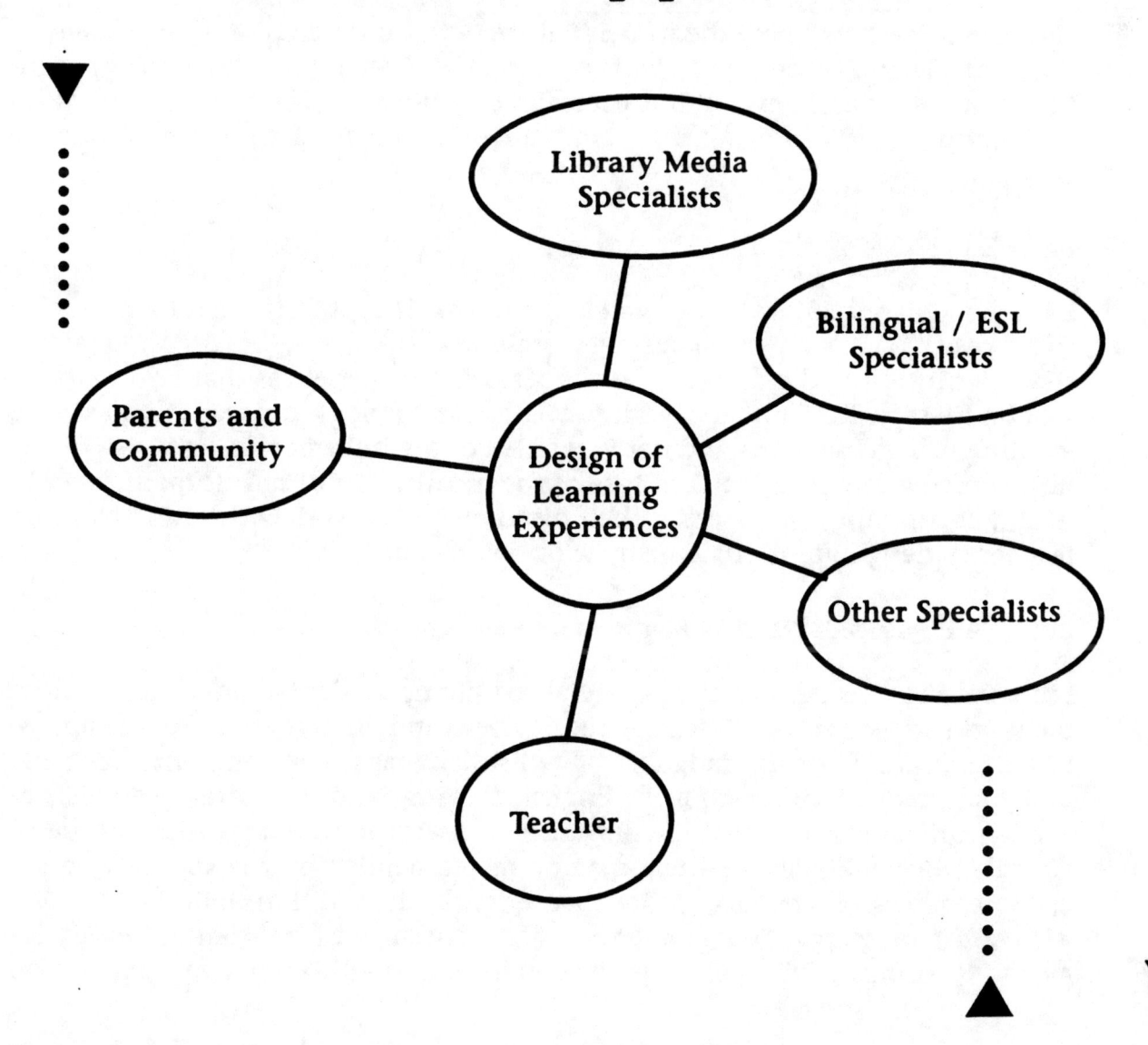

- Library Media Specialists
- Bilingual / ESL Specialists
- Other Specialists
- Teacher
- Parents and Community
- Design of Learning Experiences

A Team Approach to Information Literacy

The Curricular Planning Team

The complex task of preparing all students to be information literate suggests a team approach. This collaboration includes library media specialists, classroom teachers, bilingual/ESL specialists and other specialists, and parents as needed. Teaching students a search process isolated from the curriculum is useless. Similarly, requiring students to perform research without teaching the search process frustrates the students as they face an ocean of information. The team can combine content and process in such a way that planning is enhanced and students are more engaged. Each member of the team brings to the table a unique set of skills. What are these skills?

<u>Classroom teachers</u>

Classroom teachers know the individual strengths and needs of each student in the class. They are the experts in the curricula for their grade level. They identify the content and develop the strategies to implement instruction. They also are responsible for ensuring that their students achieve identified performance standards.

<u>Library media specialists</u>

Library media specialists bring knowledge and skills about information and ways to process it. They are curriculum generalists who know resources and creative strategies for using them, and have a repertoire of experiences that lead to information literacy. They understand information technology and ways to maximize learning using computers and networks. All of the information resources of the library media center, as well as those of the broader worlds of information within and beyond the school, are at their disposal as they work with each classroom teacher to design appropriate instruction for all students.

<u>Bilingual/ESL specialists and aides</u>

Bilingual/ESL specialists help to assess and define students' language development and any specific individual needs. They can help to determine the appropriate mix of primary language, English-language development, specially designed academic instruction in English (SDAIE), and mainstream English to use in various instructional circumstances. Learning resources that can be of special value to English learners may be recommended by the specialist, especially resources in languages other than English. In addition, bilingual specialists are the most qualified people to ask for assistance in translating terminology and learning activities used to develop information literacy concepts.

Bilingual aides can help to communicate with students and guide activities in their primary language(s). They should be involved in all of the planning so that they can understand the objectives, content, and strategies for engaging students and the anticipated outcomes. In the development of information literacy for all students, bilingual aides may work most closely with individuals who will have important contributions to make in modeling information literacy in the students' primary language.

Other specialists

When counselors, art and music teachers, computer coordinators, or teachers of other disciplines join the planning team, an original textbook-based unit can expand to become cross-disciplinary and engaging. A history unit takes on elements of science, math, and the humanities. A math unit becomes the use of numbers and equations to solve a real world problem. A literature unit looks at the time period of a novel to increase understanding. These specialists may also have their own learning objectives to integrate into a learning experience. The computer coordinator may introduce Internet resources, help students learn to transfer information into databases, or encourage the use of e-mail. The counselor may be concerned with career possibilities, helping young people improve family relationships, and/or exploring current teen problems in context.

Parents and community

Parents and community members may also be able to play an effective role in some aspects of planning for information literacy. Business leaders, social workers, political leaders, parent organizations, and community agencies, are but a few of the possible resources available as instructional activities are made more relevant to the problems faced in the real world.

Students

In student-centered approaches, students become an important part of the planning team. Under the guidance of the adults they will create the engaging problems as a part of an entire classroom investigation.

Planning Approaches: Traditional and Constructivist

In the past ten years, a fundamental change in the way teachers might design and deliver instruction has been proposed and popularized by a variety of groups including the Coalition for Essential Schools. Viewed as part of the restructuring movement, the approach labeled "constructivist" draws upon the work of John Dewey. The constructivist approach, also known as inquiry-based, places the student at the center of instructional planning, asking each student to assume a much greater role in designing, carrying out, and assessing educational experiences. As the student creates questions to explore and projects to do, the teacher and library media specialist serve as facilitators rather than directors of a learning experience. The following lists contrast the characteristics of the traditional approach with those of the constructivist view:

Traditional Approach	Constructivist Approach
Behaviorist	Constructivist
Teacher designed	Student designed
Teacher directed	Teacher as facilitator
Direct teaching of concepts	Student creates own mental models
Textbook/lecture method	Project-based learning
Resource-based teaching	Resource-based learning

While there is a wide variety of interpretations of both traditional and constructivist approaches, a purist in the traditional approach might:

1. Design goals and objectives very carefully.
2. Design learning activities so that every learner can and will achieve the objectives.
3. Be in charge of every learning activity to see that the learning and the learner progress as planned.
4. Evaluate progress along the predesigned path.

Library media specialists have often felt left out of the traditional approach to instruction because teachers saw little need for materials over and beyond those carefully designed to achieve specified objectives, be those textbook, workbook, multimedia kit, or computer package.

On the other end of the spectrum, teachers employing the constructivist approach might:

1. Guide students in their own creation of an engaging problem, usually connected to the real world. The problem might be for an individual, a small group, or an entire class or school and could take a week, a month, or an entire year to solve.
2. Use the inquiry process or scientific method to help students design learning activities that will explore the engaging problem, usually drawing upon a wide variety of school and community resources and building upon a wide variety of disciplines.
3. Facilitate every learning activity to help students progress through the inquiry.
4. Help students design an authentic assessment, often in the form of a rubric that would serve as a signpost of not only what the student knows, but what the student can do.

Library media specialists encountering the constructivist approach might find themselves in the center of a unit as the students begin to seek resources in the school, the community, through library networks, and from the Internet to begin trying to solve their problem. Difficulties may arise because problems may not be tailored to materials already held by the library media center.

In today's world of education, independent-minded teachers tend to adopt teaching styles that may range anywhere along the continuum of traditional to constructivist methods and may not always be consistent from one learning experience to another. Other teachers might explore several methods over time and adopt a single teaching style deviating very little as time passes.

With the development of massive information infrastructures in schools, connecting classrooms and libraries to the Internet, distance education, and networking, the possible menu of teaching and learning methods has increased exponentially, and with this increase, the need for information literacy. The possibilities are exciting, yet so overwhelming, that it is difficult for any single teacher to be in command of every methodology that would benefit learning. Thus, a team approach in which teachers, library media specialists, and other specialists collaborate, seems appropriate.

Collaborative Planning of Traditional Units

Few teachers or students would begin a cross-country trip without a map. They know they must have a destination in mind and a general idea of the route they will follow. The search process is the road map to successful research. Classroom teachers, library media specialists, bilingual/ESL specialists, and students are encouraged to study the process and take from it those ideas that seem most useful to plan their own trips. Side trips and excursions to new and exciting destinations are encouraged as long as the goal remains the same (well-informed, thoughtful research, and problem-solving. The following steps are some suggestions for team members as they proceed to design, implement, and evaluate an instructional unit together. A graphic representing this collaboration follows the discussion.

Step 1: Brainstorming a Curricular Unit

At the initial planning session, the classroom teacher, the library media specialist, and other specialists can brainstorm exciting alternatives for the planned unit. Each member of this curricular teaching team brings a special level of knowledge and expertise. Using the content and process objectives and the time line, the curricular planning team determines the structure of the learning experience and what kinds of outcomes they might expect. They brainstorm about the product, and generate ideas for several alternative assignments. One assignment can be chosen at this meeting, or the teacher can reflect on the brainstormed list and make the choice later.

Step 2: Developing the Unit

When the team is ready to start planning the unit, they will use a research planning sheet or keep notes based on the Curricular Partnership Planning Model. Together they briefly describe the unit and the product. Then they write objectives for content (subject area) and process (information literacy competencies).

Specialists on the team will have their own interests and will want to integrate these into the planning. These may be listed in terms of teacher objectives or student objectives. Then the team divides the responsibilities for the unit. They decide what each will do before the students begin, what and when each will teach, where the learning activities will occur, and who will be responsible for follow-up.

Often, the team will be using unit descriptions already prepared in textbooks, curriculum guides, or state standards. The essential question is how to adapt what others have written or envisioned for the students at hand. At times, the team will be combining several preprinted unit descriptions into a single educational experience they might title an integrated unit. At other times, they may have to start from scratch, building the unit from the beginning.

Step 3: Preparing Guidelines for Students

After all the plans are made, the classroom teacher and the specialists may each prepare guidelines for students. The guidelines should include the objective, stated in terms that the students can understand, a schedule with daily goals, a description of the final product; and evaluation criteria. The guidelines will give students a structure and focus, and will raise the likelihood of their success.

Step 4: Implementing the Unit

When working with students in the library, each member of the teaching team should model the search process. Each can be a facilitator to the students at each stage of the search process rather than a passive observer or mere disciplinarian. As Emerson is often quoted, "What you do speaks so loudly, I can't hear what you say." The team must recognize their different areas of strength as they guide students toward success. These strengths come from the native talents of each team member as well as those unique to their training. Team teaching rather than "each-take-a-turn" teaching allows more individuals or student groups to have an adult facilitator.

Step 5: Evaluating the Unit

The entire curriculum teaching team is involved in the evaluation of the products students create and the experience as a whole. Students may also be involved in the evaluation as they reflect on how well they accomplished the objectives set out at the beginning of the unit both personally and as a class. This is a good time for the team to note suggestions for the future so that the next time the unit is taught, materials, resources, technology, or procedures will be in place.[1]

Collaborative Planning (Traditional Method)

Create Partnership

Library Media Specialists
Primary Expertise
 Materials
 Technology
 Process
Secondary Expertise
 Content

Other Specialists
Primary Expertise
 Strategies
 Special Content
Secondary Expertise
 Materials
 Technology

Classroom Teachers
Primary Expertise
 Content
 Process
Secondary Expertise
 Materials
 Technology

↓

Brainstorm a Curricular Unit

↓

Goals and Objectives

Learning Activities

Lesson Plans
(Guidelines for Students)

Evaluation Strategies

↓

Responsibilities
Library Media Specialists; Other Specialists; Classroom Teachers

↓

Joint Implementation

↓

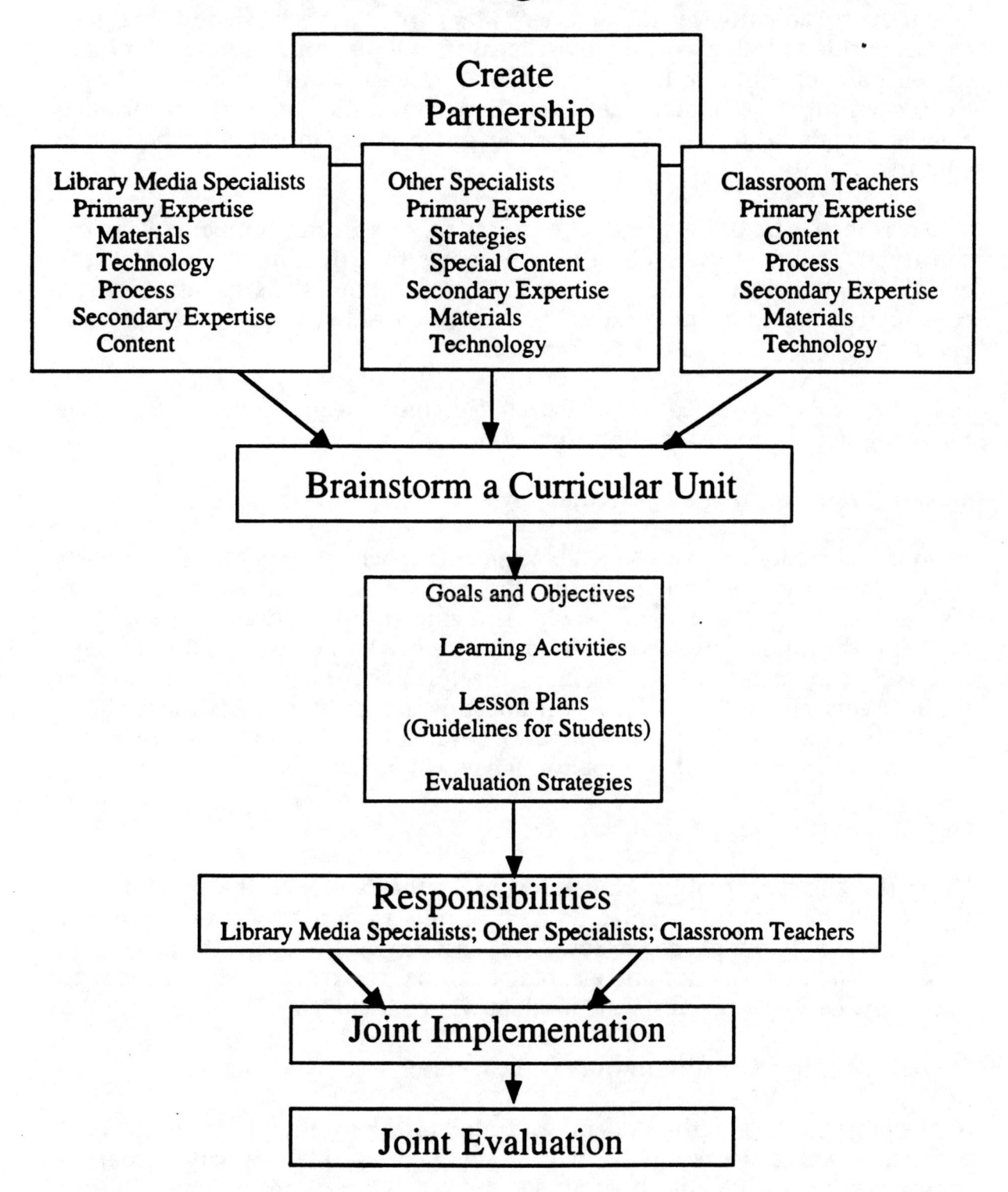

Joint Evaluation

Figure. 5: Curricular Partnership Planning Model

Collaboration to Create a Constructivist Unit

When the collaborative team of teachers, library media specialists and other specialists decide to follow constructivist ideas in the planning of instruction, the students are brought into the planning cycle very early in the process. At first, the process might seem quite messy and time consuming, but with practice, the students would begin to understand their primary responsibility for becoming educated.

Whereas in the traditional unit, the search process is one component, in the constructivist unit, the search process becomes the structure upon which the entire educational experience is created. Figure 6 shows the steps in creating a constructivist-based learning experience. Figure 6 should be studied and compared with Figure 5 to note the differences.

Using Figure 6 as a model, the collaborative planning team would engage in the following steps or some variation thereof.

Step 1: Brainstorming a Curricular Unit

In an initial session, the teachers, library media specialists, and other specialists might plan the content and skills the students would be held accountable. At a second meeting, the students would be included to help design an engaging problem which takes into account student interests while insuring that content and skills can be mastered. Together, the team will plan what the students should know and be able to do. At this meeting, not only the engaging problem will be designed but also a rubric/model of evaluative criteria that will help students know precisely how their performance will be evaluated.

Step 2: Developing the Unit

Using the engaging problem and the search process model, the students and their facilitators would design activities for finding the necessary resources and creating the activities needed to solve the problem. At this stage, the product of the investigation is defined and elaborated so that the requisite skills needed to master the content and create the product will be included.

Step 3: Working as a Community of Learners

As the project is begun, the students and adults work together to investigate the problem - sometimes as individuals, sometimes as small or large groups - sometimes in an investigative mode and at other times receiving direct instruction on the skills needed to solve the problem. The library media specialist and the teachers will assist the students in accessing needed resources to carry out the project. At this point, the work of reading, viewing, listening,

Collaborative Planning (Constructivist Method)

Create Partnership

Library Media Specialists
 Primary Expertise
  Materials
  Technology
  Process
 Secondary Expertise
  Content

Students
 Primary Expertise
  Native Ability
  Interests
 Secondary Expertise
  Materials
  Technology

Classroom Teachers
 Primary Expertise
  Content
  Process
 Secondary Expertise
  Materials
  Technology

Other Specialists
 Primary Expertise
  Strategies
  Special Content
 Secondary Expertise
  Materials
  Technology

Brainstorm a Curricular Unit

What we want to know.

How we will find out.

What materials and technology we will use.

What product we will create.

How we will be evaluated.

Responsibilities
Library Media Specialists; Students; Other Specialists; Classroom Teachers

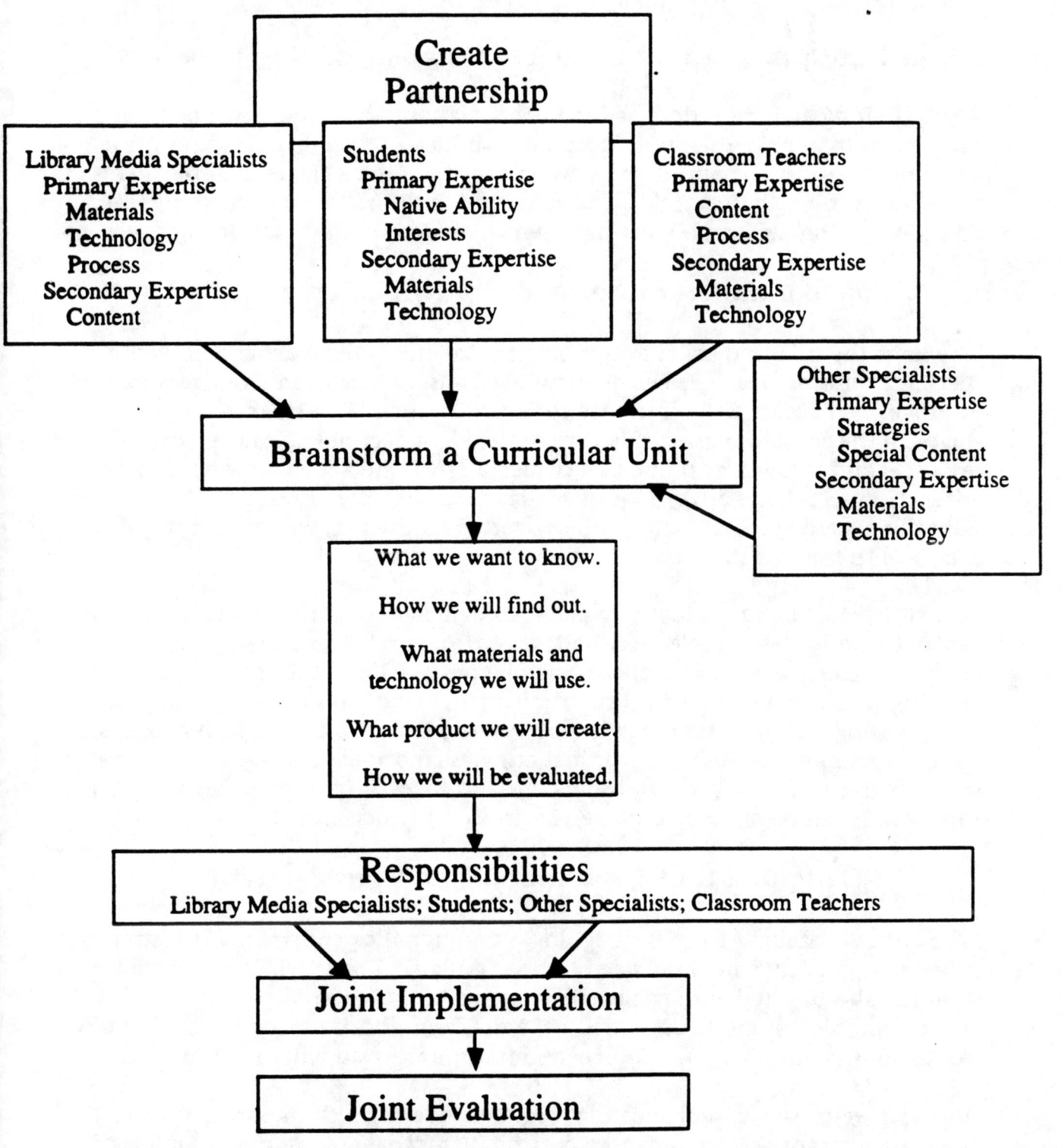

Joint Implementation

Joint Evaluation

Figure 6: Collaborative Planning (Constructivist Method)

investigating, thinking, analyzing, and concluding occupies a major part of the unit. These activities may take place in the classroom, the library media center, other parts of the school, or in the community. The products will be designed and developed.

Step 4: Participating in a Culminating Activity and Assessing the Results

A culminating activity is designed in such a way that the whole will be greater than the sum of its parts. Students might conduct a fair, a demonstration, a re-enactment, an oral report, or show web pages they have created. Assessments are made as this activity unfolds, and at the conclusion, the entire teaching team and the students reflect on what has been learned and how it was learned.

Collaboration for Improved Academic Achievement

Why take the time and effort to combine the talents of the teacher with various specialists or other teachers on instructional units? There is only one reason: to improve the educational experience for every learner. The teacher could have stayed in the classroom using existing resources and technology there, but as the resources and technology of the library media center are added, new possibilities arise. However, these are only possibilities, not guaranteed results. How carefully the experience is designed and supported by each teaching team member is critical to the overall success.

Much depends on the initial design. If students are sent to the library media center to find a few simple facts and record them on a worksheet, very little learning is likely to result. Students may be observed as cutting, copying, and clipping items for reports with little thought. They might spend most of their time creating a product that may be glitzy but of little substance. In both cases, the collaboration has failed. The initial task design can encourage, almost force, students to use a wide variety of materials and then think their way through a variety of issues before they can even begin to construct some kind of product.

Designing Units: Traditional and Constructivist

Whether the teaching team is designing a traditional or constructivist learning experience, student's interests need to be stimulated. They will need to realize what lies ahead, whether they have participated in the lesson design or not. The way the problem is constructed will have major implications for the quality of work and what information resources and technologies students are likely to use.

How can we construct problems that require students to think rather than just copy down an answer? How can we pose problems that engage student interest? For example, if students are given a worksheet that requires them to list a few facts about a bird from reference sources, they will seek the "right answer" from a reference source or Internet site. Likewise if they are given a short paper to write and must use three periodical articles and two books for their sources, they are likely to do exactly the minimum even when the available information pool is extremely rich.

Assignments or problems that take advantage of the deepening information pool have a few common characteristics. They:

- Lead to the mastery of a certain body of content knowledge;
- Encourage exploration of content knowledge beyond the minimum;
- Grab student attention and interest;
- Bring the student into contact with a variety of ideas, issues, problems, solutions, questions, etc.;
- Promote the use of a wide variety of information sources;
- Help students grapple with the ideas they locate;
- Allow for student creativity as they try to solve problems or dilemmas;
- Encourage thinking over mindless copying; and
- Allow students to communicate their work in a variety of formats.

The following units from various curricular areas are examples of assignments/projects/problems that have been designed both traditionally and constructively. Regardless of approach, each problem should have most of the above characteristics. Students should not be able to locate a single answer in a single source to complete the quest. A variety of subject areas have been included here. The reader might test each example against the characteristics of a good problem above and improve upon them.

Business Education

Traditional	Constructivist
• Compare advertising techniques and results from 100 years ago and today.	• Community leaders in today's newspaper are worried that our generation is a slave to advertising techniques. Are we really any more susceptible to advertising than those living 100 years ago, and do we really think any less for ourselves?
• Compare the research and development programs of two major corporations.	• Two major corporations are dominating the economy of our community. Some are afraid that these corporations will not be here very long unless their research and development programs are keeping the company on the cutting edge of the competition. What are both companies doing in research and development and is a bright future a realistic scenario?
• Develop a business plan for starting your own company.	• The biggest complaint we have as a class about our part time jobs is that we are all working for someone else and at low wages. Can we do something to break this cycle and start working for ourselves?
	• Last night on television, commentators were saying that the small business is the strength of the economy. Can children or teenagers design and create a viable small business and prepare to create such enterprises for our future? What kinds of companies might we design and actually create?

Consumer and Homemaking Education

Traditional	Constructivist
• Judge the merits of a group of consumer products.	• There is so much hype about which brand of athletic shoe we should all be wearing. Is there really any difference between the top three brands of shoes and the less expensive brands on the market?
• Analyze the diets in a variety of ethnic cultures. How healthy is each diet according to our government's definition of healthy?	• One of our new classmates is Hmong and is not used to eating the types of food we have in our cafeteria. What is the difference between the food eaten in a Hmong home in Southeast Asia and food we eat every day? Is one diet more "nutritious" than another?
• Compare the fashions of 50 years ago with those of today.	• The drama coach has asked our class to perform a play with a setting of 50 years ago and the costumes will need to be designed.
• Compare a typical day of a mother living in Colonial America with the typical day of a modern business woman. What are the similarities and the differences?	• In a discussion in class, we found that a number of the student's mothers are trying to balance a full day of work in addition to the challenges of family life. Has the movement for "the career woman" backfired? Who is better off? The career woman of today or the housewife of yesteryear?

English/Language Arts

Traditional

• Examine the features of a publication such as a newspaper or magazine and then create a new design. How does restructuring page design affect what readers get from the information presented?

• Compare historical nonfiction and fiction. Analyze the similarities and differences.

• In *Roll of Thunder, Hear My Cry* what divides communities, neighborhoods, and families?

Constructivist

• The school newspaper design has a very tired look and our class has just volunteered to do something about it. How can we create something students would be interested in and that might be entered in the state design contest just announced?

• The movie Pocahontas has been seen by millions but does it have any basis in historical fact. Could we create a video that might be closer to what really happened?

• After reading *Roll of Thunder, Hear My Cry:* What kinds of issues would so divide our community, our families, and our neighborhoods that we would try to solve by violence or war? What are some peaceful means of solving the difficult problems we face?

Foreign Language

Traditional

• Plan a trip to a foreign country.

• Plan a celebration for a particular country's holiday.

Constructivist

• Our high school band has been invited to visit Great Britain and participate in an international music festival. How will we be able to participate? What will we need to plan? What finances will we need?

• Our sister school on the Internet in Japan has asked us to participate in their celebration of the new year. What is involved, and how might we share this celebration as a school and community?

Health and Physical Education

Traditional

- Explore the symptoms and diagnosis of a disease in a successful case or in an unsuccessful case. What went right? What went wrong?

- Develop an advertising campaign to promote health and physical fitness for two different audiences, e.g., your parents, your age group.

Constructivist

- Through no fault of his own, one of our classmates has just become HIV positive. What are the prospects for his life as compared to Ryan White's

- A community newspaper survey has just determined that drug use among young people in the community is on the rise. What can our class do about this problem?

History-Social Science

Traditional

- Reconstruct an event from history and dramatize it.

- Predict the role of women in the society of 2150 AD in a country other than your own.

- How did the background and cultural roots of the English affect how they recreated a new society in Colonial America?

- Create a report/presentation on a significant landmark in the United States. Why was it designated as an important place/thing? How has it survived over the years?

Constructivist

- The community theater group came to our class and said it is the 150th anniversary of the rescue of the Donner Party and wonders if we could help create and perform a presentation for the Historical Society?

- After the mayoral election in our community, the mother of one of our students who was a candidate claimed that no woman could be elected mayor in our town. We would like to investigate this notion, since we don't really believe that.

- If the English culture affected the society of Colonial America, how do our own background and cultural roots affect the community in which we live?

- In our town, a seventy-year-old landmark, a civic clubhouse, has been earmarked for destruction. Is it worth saving? If so, how could it be saved?

Industrial and Technology Education

Traditional	Constructivist
• Prepare a plan to bring a new invention into the general marketplace.	• Our class received notice from the state inventor's society that it will be holding a state-wide contest for inventions that can be taken to market. They have challenged us to participate.
• Demonstrate the difference between internal combustion and electric engines.	• The local car dealer has just received shipment of the first commercial electric car. He would like us to test it out and create a local ad targeted at the audience for this vehicle. Can we help?

Science

Traditional	Constructivist
• Trace the history of the explanations for why the Tacoma Narrows Bridge (in the state of Washington) failed. Why did the reported cause change over time?	• The bridge in our community connecting two major parts of town became unsafe last year because of an earthquake. A plan is now developing to retrofit the bridge. How can any bridge be designed to withstand a heavy earthquake? Are there examples of bridges that have withstood a major quake? Why have they survived? What could our community learn from other designs?
• The rat is common to many parts of the world. Compare the rats in any two countries of the world. What are the differences in the impact they have on the people and the environment.	• The most annoying animal problem our community faces is _____. What have other communities, nations or areas done to control an animal problem? Is it possible for natural enemies to co-exist? How could that happen? What examples from other places might be used to solve our problem?

Assessing Teaching and Learning

Checking Plans for Instructional Activities: Assessing Teaching

How can we, as teachers, library media specialists, bilingual/ESL specialists, or other specialists be sure that we are on the right track as we plan instructional activities and projects? It may be helpful to use the following checklist before we start teaching.

How will this assignment contribute to the development of information literacy?

- Based on curricular goals and objectives or motivated by student need?
- Essential and timely to the task at hand?
- Designed to create and sustain interest in learning?
- Worthy of the time and effort required?
- Developmentally appropriate for the class or group?
- Tailored to meet adequately the varying capabilities of the class or group, with each student challenged yet capable of completing the requirements?
- Relevant to students' cultural, social, economic, and personal circumstances?
- Planned to ensure the availability of a sufficient quantity of suitable resources in all languages?
- Designed so that specific learning skills, reference tools, and /or research techniques are introduced and reinforced by the classroom teacher, the bilingual/ESL specialist, and the library media specialist?
- Clearly and completely communicated so that students know what is expected of them?[2]

You might also wish to consider these important questions:

- Would you willingly, eagerly, and happily welcome this assignment, or is it humdrum, mechanical, unchallenging work?
- Have you done this assignment yourself? Have you ironed out the pitfalls and problems?
- How will you involve the students in evaluation of the process and the product?

It is essential that students have assignments that are precisely defined, carefully circumscribed, and within their competence to perform. It is also essential that the resources necessary to complete the assignment are readily available.

Performance-Based Assessment: Assessing Learning

In performance-based assessment, students are asked to perform specific behaviors that are to be assessed. For example, to demonstrate a mastery of historical fact, students may debate an issue as if they were Thomas Jefferson. To prove that they can write, students might produce a writing sample; they might also plan and assemble portfolios of their work to demonstrate their competence or progress in a specific area. Consider the following factors as performance-based assessment plans are formulated:

• **The search process is a performance.** It is a series of behaviors a searcher performs in response to a need for information.

• **Both the process and the product of research can be assessed.** To document and analyze the process, searchers use a search process journal as they continually assess how their actions are moving them toward attaining their information objectives. Assessment of the products of research is as varied as the products themselves, such as debates, dramatic performances, visual presentations, or research papers.

• **The search process is applicable for either portfolio or authentic assessment models.** A portfolio is a sample of representative student work collected over time. Portfolios are as diverse as the teachers and students who collaborate to design what will go into them. An assessment portfolio in any curriculum area might include the student's search process journal as well as the product or other result of research in that subject area. In the authentic assessment model, emphasis is on the student demonstrating what can be done such as fixing a defective engine, speaking fluently in another language, performing an act of community service, performing a piece of music, or exhibiting at a learning fair.

• **The searcher, the classroom teacher, the library media specialist, and any other specialists should all be involved in the assessment.** Each has a unique perspective and distinct criteria that will govern the assessment. The combination of their individual perspectives will determine the outcome. Through involvement in the assessment process, students are responsible and accountable for their own learning.

Consider the following questions that could be asked regarding a student project. Which questions are appropriate to a specific project? Who will do the evaluation? The classroom teacher alone? The library media specialist alone? A joint evaluation?

1. How clearly was the problem expressed?
2. Were appropriate key words, concepts, and names identified?
3. What search strategies were used?
4. Were appropriate sources consulted?
5. How was the information evaluated?
6. In the final product, were all sources adequately identified?
7. Was copied material appropriately cited? Was copied material logically and effectively integrated into the project? Is there evidence that the work presented is the work of the student rather than friends or family?
8. What was the quality of the content and presentation of the product? (For a written paper, this might include accuracy of information, sound reasoning, suitable structure, transitions between ideas, grammar, spelling, and usage)
9. How was the material presented? How suitable was the presentation for the intended audience?
10. What evidence was there of the student's creativity in approaching or thinking about the problem and creating a product?
11. Was technology appropriately used for the project research and presentation?

The Bottom Line: Assessing the Teaching/Learning Experience

The following questions might be included in the assessment of the entire process:

1. Has student learning increased enough to justify the time and effort expended?
2. Were students engaged in the learning process?
3. Has the world of information and technology been explored?
4. Has information literacy increased significantly?
5. Have the instructional strategies used to build student skill and content knowledge been appropriate and targeted?
6. From the perspective of standards for content and skills acquisition, have the students acquired both the knowledge and the skills needed to prepare for the real world?

NOTES

1. The section on collaborative planning of traditional units is adapted from Stripling, Barbara K. and Judy M. Pitts, *Brainstorms and Blueprints*, Libraries Unlimited, 1988, p. 24-26.
2. This checklist is adapted from Davies, Ruth Ann, "How Feasible Is Your Assignment?" *Emergency Librarian* XI, September-October, 1983, p. 13.

Chapter 5

The Instructional Process: Resource-Based Learning

Information-Rich Environment

Settings	Learning Resources
Home	People
School	Places
Community	Print
Libraries	Technology

Resource-Based Learning

Definition

Information literacy or knowing how to learn, is a basic survival skill for the 21st century. The development of information literacy must be placed within the context of the overall learning process and linked with the processes of thinking, writing, discussing, problem solving, and decision making. Information literacy can be achieved when schools are restructured around resource-based learning and resource-based teaching.

Resource-based teaching and resource-based learning are not synonymous. In resource-based teaching, teachers use a variety of resources such as newspapers, library books, video, computer software, and online databases to facilitate their teaching and in the design of instruction for their students. In resource-based learning, students may access the same resources, but the focus is on what the students are doing with these resources to facilitate their own learning.

Resource-based learning requires restructuring of:

- The learning environment,
- The learning process,
- The role of the student,
- The role of the teacher, and
- The relationship between student and teacher.

Facilitator of learning is now the fundamental role of the teacher, the library media specialist and other specialists in the school. In order to facilitate student learning, the curricular planning team has three primary functions:

- Structure the learning environment,
- Guide student learning, and
- Track and assess student learning.

Structure the Learning Environment

The environment must be structured to ensure that the inquiry, investigation, and development of information literacy are nurtured, and that the optimum opportunity for student learning exists. The teaching team:

- Establishes objectives based on curriculum frameworks,
- Works with students to establish learning objectives and identify information needs,
- Selects or previews available resources to ensure suitability,
- Designs learning activities and experiences or task-oriented assignments to

connect students with resources in a meaningful way, and
- Has high expectations and gives specific instructions.

Facilitate Student Learning

The teaching team works together to facilitate and elevate student learning. Through careful collaboration and in thoughtful interaction with students, they:

- Question students to stimulate their thinking,
- Guide students to identify their own information needs,
- Offer prompts to facilitate understanding, and
- Assist at all stages of the research process to ensure that students receive help with learning when and where necessary.

Track and Assess Student Learning

Both the teaching team and the learner are engaged in the assessment of learning. Together they:

- Record students' levels of cognitive processing and the development of information skills,
- Evaluate how learning resources are used,
- Evaluate the achievement of learning objectives, and
- Evaluate research products and process.

The graphic on the following page provides a visual analysis of resource-based learning with the student at the center.[1]

Resource-Based Learning: What Does It Look Like?

Learning Resources

Technology
Video/ITV
Filmstrips
Audio
Computers
Videodiscs
CD ROM
Telecommunications
Other

Print
Books
Magazines
Newspapers
Textbooks
Pamphlets
Maps
Other

Places
Universities
Schools
Libraries
Museums
Zoos
Communities
Other

People
Classroom teachers
Library media specialists
Parents
Experts
Resource people
Other

Resource-Based Learning

Student at center
Uses resources to broaden learning base

Classroom teachers and library media specialists function as facilitators of learning:

Structure learning environment...
- Establish learning objectives
- Select/preview resources to ensure suitability for learning/learners
- Design learning experiences
- Set task-oriented assignments
- Create engaging problems

Facilitate student learning...
- Question to stimulate thinking
- Guide students to identify their own information needs
- Prompt to facilitate understanding
- Assist to ensure that students receive help with learning when/where necessary

Track and assess student learning...
- Record student's level of cognitive processing
- Record development of information literacy skills
- Evaluate how students use learning resources
- Evaluate student achievement of learning objectives
- Evaluate products

Resources in the Home, Community, School, and Beyond

If learning is to be resource-based, students must be aware of the wealth of resources available to them in all areas of their environment. We must encourage all students to explore a wide range of learning resources that encompasses the home, the community, the school, and beyond. Rather than being dependent on the teacher and the textbook, students should be able to locate the information they need wherever it may be.

The resources from home, both tangible and intangible, that students bring into the classroom represent both their heritage and knowledge base. The community in which the student lives can provide distinct resources and avenues of information. When we encourage and assist students in identifying community resources and developing an understanding of how these can facilitate and support the search for information, we are also demonstrating that information resources that originate in their homes and community are valued and relevant. In the school, the library media center should function as a learning channel through which students have access to the vast information sources within and beyond the school.

Resources in the Home

Few children think of their homes as rich sources of information. Indeed, even teachers often overlook the home as a curricular resource.

In studies conducted by Luis Moll and Norma Gonzalez, research teams, usually composed of a teacher and an ethnographer, visited the homes of second-language learners as observers to identify the kinds of information resources and networks to which these students had access. They discovered rich "funds of knowledge" with obvious potential connections to curriculum as shown in Table 1.[2]

Table 1
A Sample of Household Funds of Knowledge

Agriculture and mining	Economics	Household management	Material & scientific knowledge	Medicine	Religion
Ranching and farming Horsemanship (cowboys) Animal husbandry Soil and irrigation systems Crop planting Hunting, tracking dressing Mining Timbering Minerals Blasting Equipment operation and maintenance	Business Market values Appraising Renting and selling Loans Labor laws Building codes Consumer knowledge Accounting Sales	Budgets Childcare Cooking Appliance repairs	Construction Carpentry Roofing Masonry Painting Design and architecture Repair Airplane Automobile Tractor House maintenance	Contemporary medicine Drugs First aid procedures Anatomy Midwifery Folk medicine Herbal knowledge Folk cures Folk veterinary cures	Catechism Baptisms Bible studies Moral knowledge and ethics

Information Literacy

While the sources of information listed in the table are specific to the homes of the bilingual students in the geographic setting of the study, it is easy to imagine the different but equally vast funds of knowledge in the homes of students from other cultures. The study on household funds of knowledge is a reminder that the breadth of knowledge in any household is typically extensive and often ignored or underestimated by the schools. The findings of Moll have obvious implications for our consideration of information literacy for all students.

Resources in the Community

Community, as used here, serves as an icon for the world that lies both between and beyond the students' worlds of home and school. Typically, this is a world that both students and teachers take for granted and, therefore, overlook as a rich source of information. Both students and teachers must venture beyond home and school to explore and gather the wealth of information the community can provide.

Some communities may be both unique and unfamiliar to teachers and to some of the students in the school. Such differences have potential for contributing in richness and variety to the resources in the classroom. When students recognize and value the people, places, and things in their neighborhoods as sources of information, they become more effective users of information, and the worlds of all students are expanded and enriched.

Learning about the resources in one's own community also provides a basis for finding information in new places. If students know how to find the answers to questions about their own community, they are better prepared to adapt to new and unfamiliar settings.

For example, do students know:

- What newspapers or magazines are available in my home language? Where can I buy them? Are they in the public library? How can I find the library?
- How can I get information on bus routes so I can get to the library? To the museum? To the zoo? The nearest beach?
- Where do I get a driver's license? How can I study for the test?
- How do I look up a name in a telephone book? Use a ZIP code directory?
- What are the special places? Who are the special people in my community?

What questions might learners have about the communities in which they now live? With what other communities can/should the curriculum connect them? What other questions should they ask?

Making Resource Connections from Students' Homes and Communities to the School

How can we use students' funds of knowledge? Moll and his colleagues think that learning modes in students' homes may, in some regards, serve as a model for schools.

> In contrast to the households and their social networks, the classrooms seem encapsulated, if not isolated, from the social worlds and resources of the community. When funds of knowledge are not readily available within households, relationships with individuals outside the households are activated to meet either household or individual needs. In classrooms, however, teachers rarely draw on the resources of the "funds of knowledge" of the child's world outside the context of the classroom. Children in the households are not passive bystanders, as they seem in the classrooms, but active participants in a broad range of activities mediated by these social relationships. Within these contexts much of the teaching and learning is motivated by the children's interests and questions; in contrast to classrooms, knowledge is obtained by the children, not imposed by the adults.[3]

Moll describes how one teacher in his study took advantage of new knowledge that she had gained from her personal research in the homes and community of her students. Hilda Angiulo, a classroom teacher, developed a curricular unit that utilized at least seven different sources of funds of knowledge that she had discovered. The chart on the following page shows how Angiulo used her contacts with the home and the community in her classroom.[4]

Moll concludes:
> What is important is that the teacher invited parents and others in the community to contribute intellectually to the development of lessons. In total, about 20 community people visited the classroom during the semester contributing to lessons. These classroom visits were not trivial; parents and others came to share their knowledge, expertise, or experiences with the students and the teacher. This knowledge, in turn, became part of the students' work or a focus of study.
>
> Through the development of a social network for teaching, the teacher convinced herself that valuable knowledge existed beyond the classroom and that it could be mobilized for academic purposes. The teacher's role in these activities became that of a facilitator, mediating the students' interactions with text and with the social resources made available to develop their analysis, and monitoring their progress in reading and writing in two languages.[5]

▼ Chapter 5 • Resource-Based Learning

....

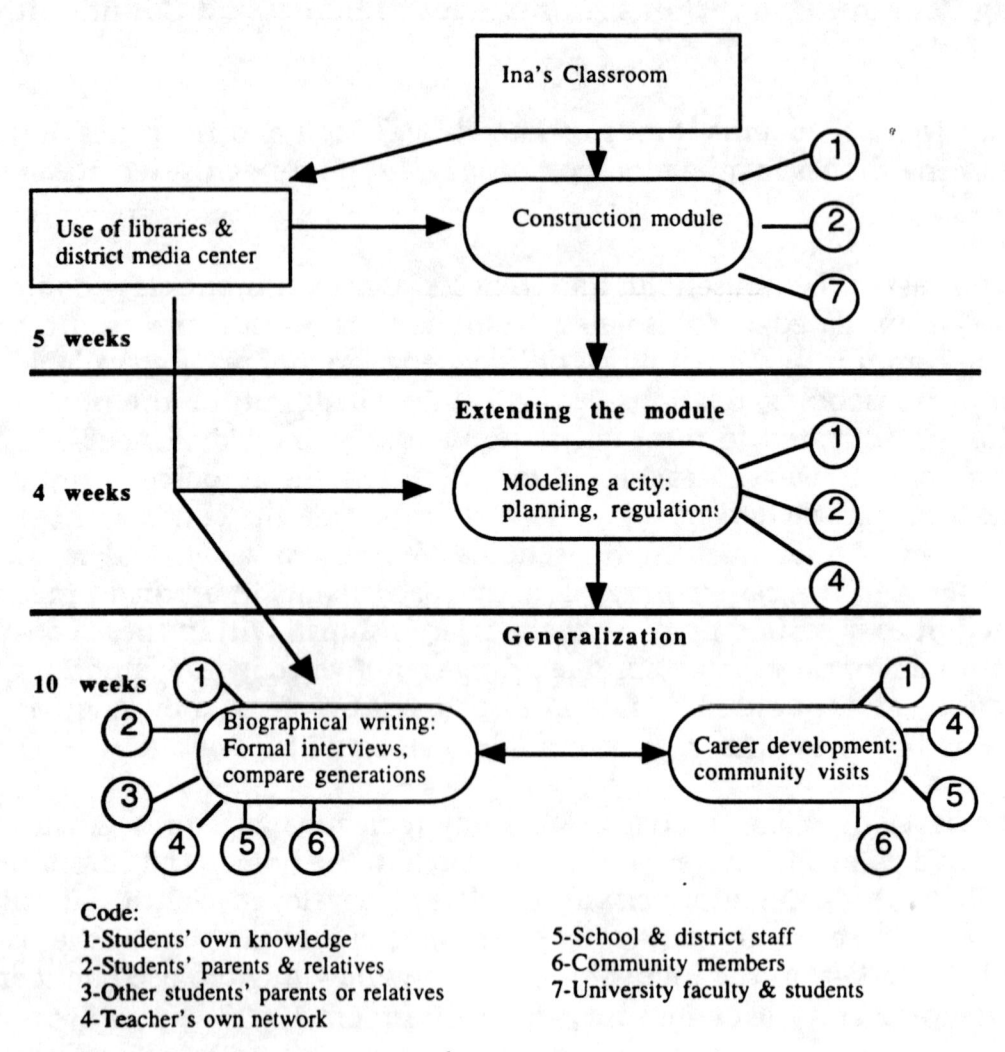

```
                          Ina's Classroom
                         ↙           ↘
        Use of libraries &  →  Construction module  — 1
        district media center                       — 2
                                    │               — 7
  5 weeks  ─────────────────────────┼──────────────────
                              Extending the module
                                    ↓
  4 weeks        →          Modeling a city:          — 1
                            planning, regulations     — 2
                                    │                 — 4
         ────────────────────────── ┼──────────────────
                               Generalization
  10 weeks  1
           2  Biographical writing:      Career development:   1
           3  Formal interviews,    ←→   community visits      4
              compare generations                              5
           4  5  6                                             6
```

Code:
1-Students' own knowledge
2-Students' parents & relatives
3-Other students' parents or relatives
4-Teacher's own network

5-School & district staff
6-Community members
7-University faculty & students

Figure 7: Community Information Sources[6]

Resources in the School

In the school, the library media center can be the channel for providing access to information. As stated in *Information Power*, the national guidelines for school library media programs: "The mission of the library media center is to ensure that students and staff are effective users of ideas and information."[7] The same document recognizes that information literacy depends to a large extent on access to information.

Today's library media center can offer a rich and varied collection of curriculum-related resources. In addition to print resources of all types, today's library media centers also have technology and media-based resources, such as videos, computer software, CD-ROM programs and connections to the Internet. The collection of the library media center should also include a wide variety of relevant resources in the primary languages of all students.

Perhaps the key access issue relates to students' awareness of and ability to use the vast array of information sources that are available both within and beyond the library media center. For some students with physical disabilities, access is often dependent on the format in which resources are available. The library media center is the focal point for developing information literacy. The library media staff is responsible for providing leadership in this area and should take into consideration the access needs of all students. They must also direct students to the world of resources beyond the library media center students if students are to experience information power.

All students must understand the purpose, resources, and organization of a library. In many countries, schools do not have library media centers, and public libraries are not as accessible as they are in the United States. Many traditional library resources may be unknown to students from those countries. Encyclopedias, dictionaries, atlases, the library catalog – all need to be introduced and explained in each student's primary language. The students need to understand that all of these resources are organized for their use, that many may be borrowed for use in their classroom or at home, and – most important – that the library media center staff is friendly and helpful.

Other access issues relate to library media center organization and cataloging. Are the resources in all languages cataloged and shelved in ways that will guide students to access them easily? Can resources in languages other than English be visibly identified? Are resources in all languages assigned classification numbers that reflect the subject of their content rather than the language in which they are written? For example, all nonfiction books about state history should have the same Dewey classification number whether they are in English, Filipino or Spanish. If all resources are shelved in order by classification number rather than by language, then all resources on the same subject will be together on the shelf. Any student looking for books on a specific subject will find *all* the books on that subject, regardless of the language in which the book is written. Students must also be able to access resources through searching appropriate subject headings, in English and other languages used in the library catalog, whether they are online or in card form. The collection should also include works in Braille, audio-books, and technology that will facilitate access and production of resources for students with disabilities.

Students' full intellectual access to resources is in many ways even more important than physical access. To provide full intellectual access to learning resources for all learners requires the cooperation of library media specialists, classroom teachers, bilingual specialists, and others. They must determine the reading and interest levels, the language abilities, and the preferred or most appropriate learning modalities for their students. Library media specialists, in collaboration with all instructional staff, are then responsible for selecting those learning resources best suited to student needs.

▼ Chapter 5 • Resource-Based Learning

The library media center staff can serve as map makers and tour guides to the information highway and the equally important side streets. From the public library to the university campus to the historical society to the Internet, today's library media programs should provide all students with richer, deeper understanding and appreciation of information resources and the satisfaction of participating with teachers, parents, and others in a learning community.

Learning Resources: People, Places, Print, Technology

Sources of information are infinite. Whether they exist in home, community, schools, or libraries, resources can be grouped into categories that help in considering how to access them. The following examples are clustered into common categories: people, places, print, technology. Each of these categories is explored briefly on the following pages.

People	*Places*	*Print*	*Technology*
Teachers	Homes	Books	Video/TV
Library media specialists	Schools	Magazines	Computers
Family	Library media centers	Newspapers	Videodiscs
Friends/Local experts	Museums	Letters	CD-ROM
Resource people	Zoos/Stores	Maps/Photos	Telecommunications
	Businesses	Posters	

People

Almost any search for information begins with people. Who are the experts? Whom do I know? Whom can I contact? All students have access to experts in their homes, schools, and communities. Business and shop owners, factory and farm workers, people who have traveled, residents in senior care facilities, bus drivers, librarians, longshoremen, students, builders, jewelers, and waiters are just a few. What kinds of information can these people provide? What do they know? What materials, tools, and information sources do they use?

How can we best access information that people can provide? Learners may have important understandings and insights about the appropriate conventions, protocols, language, and style for approaching various community members. All students will need to learn how to interview in order to access these valuable information sources within their communities and beyond.

The skills involved in interviewing build on those considered in chapters 3 and 6 on developing questions. Students will need to plan before they interview: What do they want to know? What questions will they ask? Are there questions they should not ask? What language will they use? Should they interview in bilingual teams? Will they need a translator? Should they call to make an appointment? Should they write first? Can they use online communication? How will they find the phone number or address? How will they record the information from the interview?

When seeking information from people in the community, learners may have access to rich sources of oral history. Prepared to use their primary language or a combination of languages, students can interview people whose lives and experiences reveal life in other times or other places. Equipped with tape recorders and cameras (if these are appropriate in the cultural context), they can capture the raw material for rich, personalized documentaries and first-person accounts. They have the opportunity to use people as primary sources.

▼ Students learn local history, learn oral history, develop research skills, and make a contribution to the community when they serve as official historians. Working in small groups, students can tape oral history interviews, write up the information, collect artifacts, and present their projects to the school library, local library, or museum. Students develop a more personal connection with people in the community through these activities and increase their understanding of history, historical research, and continuity and change. They gain a sense of belonging and a sense of their personal place in the evolving community. Their work is validated when it becomes a part of a permanent collection of historical research and data.[8]

Places

Many places exist as special sources of information. Museums, libraries, stores, businesses, zoos, historical societies, and government buildings are all organized for dissemination of particular kinds of information. In addition, businesses, embassies, markets, and transportation systems may provide the raw materials for information problem solving. In most communities, the public library is a primary source of information. Many public libraries offer information resources in the primary languages of the community. They also offer information in audiovisual and technology-based formats that may be more accessible than text for English learners. Bilingual librarians help students locate, evaluate, and use all of the library resources in whichever languages and formats are most appropriate. School library media specialists can work closely with the public librarians to introduce all of their students to the rich resources of the public libraries in their neighborhoods.

Community centers and places of worship can also provide information in a variety of languages and representing many viewpoints. Students of diverse backgrounds can be reassured that their teachers will value these resources for their contribution to the "funds of knowledge" and for the diversity that they may bring to the topic or question being studied.

How can students learn to recognize the potential of places that may otherwise seem mere buildings? How will they find these places? The keys to finding both people and places often lie in print resources.

Print/Graphic

One of the most common ways for teachers to access information is in print. Print sources found in the home, school, and community and in many languages are basic tools for information problem solving. On the following pages, selected types of print resources are discussed as sources of information.

Reference Sources

Reference tools provide concentrated subject matter organized for information access. We use most other materials in their entirety (e.g., read the whole book, view the entire video), but typically use reference sources to look up specific information. Alphabetical arrangement, indexes, and electronic search functions all help us to locate the exact information we need.

For all students, full access to reference resources depends on their knowing the nature and scope of the contents. Is it a comprehensive encyclopedia or an animal encyclopedia? Are the biographies those of people living today or only of people from the past? Students must also know how the content is organized. Can you look up terms in an index? Do you find an article by using alphabetical guide words at the top of the page?

These access features generally apply to reference tools in all languages. Students who develop location skills for using reference sources in one language will be able to transfer this knowledge to resources in their second language.

It is important to have reference sources in the students' primary languages to make content most accessible to them. If available, basic reference tools such as encyclopedias and dictionaries in all languages spoken by students at the school should be included in the school's collection. These materials can be available not only in the library, but can be accessed from the classroom and even from home.

Another feature of many reference sources that makes them more accessible is their visual display of content and concepts. Photographs, diagrams, maps and charts can provide information that transcends many barriers to comprehension. Even young children can be guided to use these features of reference sources to meet some of their needs for information.

Literature as a Source of Information

Because much of literature is fiction, we often overlook its potential to provide information. Many great literary works are nonfiction (e.g., biography, first-person accounts of historic events and travels, and documentaries of diverse cultures around the world). But all literature, both fiction and nonfiction, can help the reader put isolated information into context and develop new insights about information gathered from other sources. Students who read a biography or a work of historical fiction may find and comprehend information with increased understanding and a greater sense of its relevance to their own lives. It is obvious that these characteristics can apply to literature in any language.

Traditional literature or folklore is generally recognized as conveying the values, customs and characteristics of cultural groups. Folklore (i.e., stories passed from one generation to another as part of an oral tradition) is, therefore, another source of information. All students can contribute stories from their cultures and learn from the stories of others. Picture books and illustrated books provide opportunities to glean information that goes beyond text. Learning to read an illustration or photograph is an important information skill. Literature also provides models for writing. Works like biographies, first-person narratives, alphabet books, and the like, demonstrate creative ways to communicate or present information.

Because literature is a source of information that affects our understanding of others and helps to shape and influence our attitudes, we must select literature that reflects the cultural diversity of both the student body and the larger society. Junko Yokota's article titled, "Issues in Selecting Multicultural Children's Literature," identifies five important criteria:

- Cultural accuracy, both of detail and of larger issues,
- Rich in cultural details,
- Authentic dialogue and relationships,
- In-depth treatment of cultural issues, and
- Inclusion of members of a 'minority group' for a purpose.[9]

The best of the world's literature can provide both information and inspiration. Presenting literature in both English and students' other primary languages can help them to broaden their information base and enrich their vocabularies as they develop a lifelong appreciation of literature.

Newspapers and Magazines

Newspapers and magazines, found in both homes and libraries, are important sources of information. In addition to recording circumstances and events, they reflect the perspectives, cultures, and languages of the community to which they are targeted. Students can use a variety of newspapers to gather and analyze information and recognize different points of view. Their access to newspapers can add valuable information and perspectives.

Students also can contribute to newspapers. Letters to the editor are a vehicle for using information to express a point of view, persuade, or merely inform the community. Special features, like the "Voices" pages in the *Los Angeles Times*, may offer an opportunity for learners to tell their story. Students can report on their community-based studies in local neighborhood newspapers. Finally, school newspapers and online student-created newspapers or web pages are sources for gathering information and a medium for presenting information.

▼ Because newspapers and magazines are available in several languages, they may be more appropriate for some students than are other printed materials. In addition to stories and articles, political cartoons may be used to encourage analysis and critical thinking. . . . Students may wish [to explore] how the media influence the public. Students can then compare the accounts of news events in various newspapers and news magazines printed in English to those printed in other languages to identify the points of view or biases presented in each. . . . What they read in the newspaper can be compared with what they hear and see on television and hear on radio news broadcasts. . . . Students may respond more positively to analyzing data from a newspaper or news broadcast than to reading a textbook. They may come to a better understanding of bias in the reporting of facts when they have two concrete examples, in accessible newspaper formats, to compare and contrast. By encouraging students to read newspapers, teachers may open doors to students' interest in current affairs and the community, improve their abilities to judge information related to a problem and draw conclusions, and enhance their interest in reading.[10]

Photos, Art, and Artifacts

Visuals speak a universal language. They appeal because they communicate so much so easily – and they are personal. Even a photograph tells a story that is influenced by the intention and skill of the photographer. The relevance and utility of visual resources for learners are obvious. Students may have photographs that can be used as sources of information about the history of their families, the areas in which they grew up, the clothing, ceremonies, and foods of their culture, special events, historic places, or other aspects of their lives. Through their contacts in the community, learners may have access to agencies, clubs, businesses, museums or collections of photos that are rich with information. Local photographers, both professional and amateur, may take pleasure in sharing their photos as potential learning resources. Students can also use photography as a means to collect information for further analysis or comparison and to present information to others. The advent of the digital camera with its link to the computer allows an even greater opportunity for low-cost photography.

Artwork is another visual source of information independent of written or spoken language. Useful pieces of art such as postcards, magazines, books, posters, or paintings brought from another country are often overlooked. Students will need to learn how to read visual clues. What does the background of a photo or painting reveal? What is missing from the picture? How do the unseen elements reveal the artist's or photographer's point of view? Students can collaborate on unlocking meaning from pictures. Each learner may be able to add missing pieces to the information clues.

An artifact is defined as, "a simple object showing human workmanship." Household items, tools, clothing, jewelry, toys — things people use in daily life — have information to reveal about the people who make and use them. Students can learn to observe carefully and thoughtfully and to read the bits and pieces of stories artifacts have to tell. Learners can join teachers and other students to search their community and beyond for sources of artifacts. Both teachers and students will value things they would otherwise overlook when they consider their potential as artifacts. Artifacts, selected and organized by students as "culture clue kits," can help learners reveal information about their lives and gather information about the lives of others. Inevitably, as students work together with classmates to gather, interpret, organize and display photographs, works of art, and artifacts of all kinds, they also discover, reveal, and reflect their sense of community.

Technology Tools and Resources

Technology has had an impact on learning and information literacy in more than one way. First, it is largely video and computer, or electronic, technologies that have caused the exponential explosion in the amount of information available today. They have also provided the means to extend access to the disabled. Because these technologies have enabled storage and retrieval of amounts of information previously inconceivable, they have greatly dramatized the need for information literacy.

As teachers guide students in using technology resources effectively, they are discovering that a student-driven process for finding, evaluating and using information is essential since it is no longer appropriate or possible for all students to be "on the same page at the same time." And with the proliferation of available information, the need for critical evaluation of what is found and seen must become an ongoing part of every student's reading and viewing.

Today's technologies also encourage learners to become creators of their own information sources, not merely consumers of information in linear print format. Using information, the ultimate goal of information literacy, takes on new meaning as students design and construct video productions, web pages, and multi-media products.

In addition to recognizing the many learning opportunities that technology provides, we must also be aware that access to information becomes more restrictive as special equipment is required for accessing and using it. One of education's challenges is to ensure that all learners have equitable access to the new information technologies and competency in the skills of using them so that the habits and processes for their lifelong learning are well established. The contemporary library media center that becomes the focal and dissemination point for technology and other resources can provide equity of access to all students.

What are some of the technologies that can be used to enhance learning and promote information literacy for all? The following is a start to answering that question.

Video Technologies

Video, ITV, television and videodisc are variations of a popular technology found in both schools and homes. Clara Amador Watson, in an article entitled, "Instructional Video and English Learners," discusses the advantages of using these media for language acquisition, but her comments clearly extend to all students.

> ▼ The instructional potential of video use is characterized by the immediate communicative power of images and visual data regardless of students' primary language. Furthermore, students are immersed in authentic, real-life contexts representative of different countries and cultures across the world where ideas and concepts can be explored in a non-sequential, non-linear manner.
>
> Critical thinking skills may be developed when the use of video allows students to generate divergent and/or alternative explanations for a given idea, event, or opinion being discussed. Given the endless possibilities of people and places portrayed by video technologies, the formulation of simulations and role play scenarios can also be added to the repertoire of thinking-oriented activities and projects. Teachers and students need to reinvent their roles as active and critical viewers so that video viewing becomes a rich foundation for language development and critical thinking power."[11]

In addition to using commercially produced videos, creating their own video presentations can be a powerful learning experience for students. A camcorder can be used for interviews, oral histories, and so on, as students script their own reports, produce and videotape an historical drama/play, or develop a documentary on some local issue. Current technology makes it possible to develop closed captioned videos accessible for speakers of all languages and for the hearing-impaired.. It is also possible to develop a separate soundtrack in a student's primary language by creating a cassette tape to use instead of the original sound. All these activities should involve students in planning and researching the project before it is taped. These activities encourage language development, critical thinking, and problem-solving skills.

Students have access to television in their homes and many of the programs offer opportunities to develop information literacy. Classroom discussions can help them learn to analyze news, with teams of students monitoring the news as reported on local channels and comparing the viewpoints of different commentators and networks. English learners can contribute valuable information by viewing and commenting on news programs in their primary languages. When the same news is reported quite differently, a search for the truth can lead students to explore a variety of information sources.

Video technologies open information to different intelligences, as discussed by Howard Gardner in *Frames of Mind*. Visual intelligence, in which visual images are the immediate path to understanding, will be supported through the use of these technologies.

Media literacy, a sub-category under the information literacy umbrella, calls for all learners to be proficient in evaluating visual images for bias, opinion vs. content, gaps in information presented, etc. While this aspect of literacy covers more than visual images, it is a central component to creating critical viewers of media.[12]

Computer and Multimedia Resources

Computer technology has revolutionized the world of information in many ways. The capacity for handling and storing data has grown tangentially - with equally amazing methods for quickly retrieving that data growing with it. While the amount of available data or information has reached a point of doubling in ever shorter intervals, it is also true that humans' ability to process that information has remained fairly stable. Our brains have not kept pace with the information explosion, emphasizing the importance of helping learners develop a process for making meaning, converting information to personal knowledge, thus acquiring information literacy.

Computers have opened the arena of communication. Word processing programs assist one in creating communications easily, and fax machines and printers help to move those messages on to others. Data bases and spread sheets are easily used starting at an early age so students learn for themselves how to arrange, store, and retrieve information. For the physically challenged, these technologies may open doors to communication never before possible. By late elementary grades students regularly use these applications as tools for their learning. There are also multimedia, and hyperstacking tools, that offer a non-linear approach to presenting information and these tools become a natural link to the world of hypertext websites. Together, these basic computer applications offer all students an approach to learning quite different than traditional models. Students are ready at a young age to use a project approach to learning, with the accompanying need for a process to handle organizing their own information needs.

When a print reference book like an encyclopedia, dictionary, or atlas is transformed to a computer or CD-ROM disk, students must be prepared to use a whole new range of search strategies to locate the information they are seeking. By combining appropriate terms, they can locate in an instant information that previously required endless hours of poring over multiple sources. Because computerized reference tools allow the searcher to locate specific and detailed information, students and teachers should be encouraged to go beyond the general topic approach and to seek the information that answers a specific question or solves a specific problem.

New electronic reference tools have features that make them very accessible by all learners. Many programs have search strategies that are icon-based rather than menu-driven and so are less language dependent. Audio support allows a student to hear a word pronounced by clicking on an icon. Illustrations and full-motion video clips bring subjects to life in ways not possible with the printed page. Many electronic reference tools include dictionaries that are available as a special feature to define unfamiliar words that the student highlights; they also pronounce the word. Students enjoy exploring electronic encyclopedias and other reference tools in collaborative groups at the computer and developing vocabulary as they share their discoveries.

New multimedia technologies allow students to create and enhance reports using visuals from videodisc, video, camcorder, or television. Sound tracks can be developed and presentations recorded. Sharing the planning, development and presentation of such a multimedia program provides excellent opportunities for developing a variety of skills including expanding competency in information literacy.

Telecommunications

One of the clearest indicators that this is the Information Age, has come with recent federal initiatives naming Internet connections in the classroom as a high priority. Preparing students for their future will soon include the use of computers, modems, and telephone connections. Now, in effect, the use of telecommunications for learning is to become a basic component of classrooms along with textbooks and chalkboards. This offers opportunities for learning that builds on the use of computer applications as tools and gives new possibilities for collaborative learning and global awareness.

In the following sections, e-mail, collaborative projects, simulations, and on-line reference gathering will be discussed as ways to integrate information literacy and on-line learning. Brief real-life snapshots will demonstrate how information literacy is a part of the learning process in each case.

E-mail, electronic mail, has been used to share information between classrooms, to develop key-pal exchanges person to person, or to query experts for new information on a topic. Many teachers have found this a good starting point for young learners, as they first lead their classes with writing group letters that are posted on-line.

One elementary school formed a friendship with an engineer at the South Pole, who wrote them of the geology, weather, and general life at McMurdo Station as they became enthusiastic experts about the science and meteorology projects there. And for him, these lively students became a link with home that others gladly took over when his duty at McMurdo was over. Led by the school's librarian and the classroom teacher, these students learned more about forming good questions, collecting, and organizing the information that came from their contact, and ways to present their learning. This project led learners to maps, articles, and independent searches for more information about the polar region.

In another school, King George III (in reality a university history professor) visited a fifth grade classroom electronically, as students learned first about correct letter writing and forms of addressing royalty and then reacted to the King's demands for increased taxation for goods. When the students emotionally decided that these demands were unreasonable and couldn't be tolerated any longer, the teacher was ready to launch into teaching about the American Revolutionary War. Students had an insider's understanding of the colonists reasons from their own responses to each of the king's e-mail postings. Searching their textbooks for the background on each step of the original process, as well as their personal reactions to reading the King's missives, had fired up the students.

Collaborative data gathering is another area for on-line learning and information literacy connection. Having several classrooms from around the globe collecting data simultaneously on their local weather, led one eighth grade classroom to maps to learn where in the world the other sites were located. Charts and graphs comparing and contrasting the sites were prepared, scientific principles were sought to explain the noted differences. Students worked in small groups to learn more about the communities of the participating schools and had to decide together what their search strategies would be for this process. In a final activity, the groups presented a "snapshot" of each community and school, and talked about the weather patterns to the entire class.

In another example, a teacher in Maryland proposed a project on line. She called for other classrooms interested in water pollution to collaboratively plan a project taking water samples around the rim of the Atlantic Ocean. Responses quickly came in from classrooms in eight different countries that touch the Atlantic and scientists also wrote offering to discuss the scientific process, and be on-line experts during the water collecting - IF they would be given the results for their own research. Students helped plan the experiment, gathered the water samples, submitted the results to the scientists - and delved into answering their own questions regarding the background of the project. Participating in a "real" scientific experiment, where the results would be used for actual research, put learning into a serious mode. Their participation in accessing, organizing, evaluating, and using information gave them an opportunity to practice the skills of information literacy.

Simulations - Lawrence Livermore Laboratory in Livermore, California, has made available to K-12 students (through an 800 telephone number) access to some of their sophisticated simulation modeling programs. One of these, Geoman, was used by a primary classroom of special education students to aid them in making hypotheses and predictions. The class would change one feature of the current global landscape - melt the South Pole ice cap, cut down all the trees in South America - and would then predict what would happen. Cross-age tutors (from upper elementary) entered information into the brief program protocol and e-mailed it in. Within 24 hours, a short animated film was returned to the class account, depicting the results. Discussion centered on why their predictions were correct or not. Critical thinking was evidenced in many of the comments, and a general interest in learning more about the regions of our planet brought on more learning in geography, environmental science, zoology, etc.

On-line reference gathering is sometimes referred to as using the virtual library. There are similarities but there are also differences. With on-line resources skills search strategies are especially important because there is no classification system to aid in locating information. There are more primary source materials on-line than there are in most library collections. This increases the need to critically evaluate what is found for accuracy, bias, and completeness. Increasing quantities of images and movies have led to the creation of sub-script keywords, that allow keyword searches to identify information on these images. The same keywords can then be used to search for other resources.

In a high school classroom learning the basics of international business (including the economics of it all), students selected a commodity to "sell" to another country. The library media specialist worked with the business teacher to identify the latest statistics on the country, the active trading on each commodity, and the monetary values in American dollars. Students developed a profile projecting the success of their commodity in their chosen country. In this project, up-to-the-minute data were critical. Daily checks on their product led students to create charts and make predictions on future market values. Using these sources helped students see the importance of latest information and gave them a specific example of how information is used for business decisions.

Two classroom teachers created a collaborative Treasure Hunt that brought an Advanced Placement Spanish class and a mono-lingual Spanish second grade classroom together. The second graders needed help with information about their native countries because resources were not available at their site in Spanish. The high school classroom researched several South American countries and wrote a series of "hints" to their younger keypals. The elementary students asked family members for help about the flags, costumes, foods, and capital cities, as they tried to guess the name of the country. (Students had been placed in groups according to their native land.) Next, the high school students created multimedia projects putting their clues into the context of the actual country and sent these projects to the second grade classroom for exhibiting. All work was done in Spanish with a lot of visual images to assist learners in making meaning. Finally, the young students created hyperstacks, reporting back to their keypals what they had learned including new facts they had discovered in their process. The older students had an opportunity to use a more informal Spanish than usually was covered in their literature texts, worked extensively online to gather information about their country, and found the creation of the multimedia projects a real challenge because they had to limit words and express themselves more with images. Their concluding discussion on this project was that it was among their hardest work in high school - and the most rewarding! The younger students were so excited to be communicating with teenage students, loved the treasure hunt approach, and did their very best work to learn new facts to surprise their new colleagues. Finding information that was easily accessible, creating their own projects using scanned-in images, clip art, and text was hard work for them, but they loved having a real audience.

Information literacy in telecommunications is achieved when learners use on-line resources, access information competently, evaluate information for accuracy and pertinence, and use this information to communicate effectively. Most of all, they have an opportunity to bring about change and be creative. Learners who are able to do this have life-long skills they will need in the Information Age.

▼ Chapter 5 • Resource-Based Learning

NOTES

1. This article, written by Bonnie O'Brian, is a summary and interpretation of an earlier piece written by Carol-Ann Haycock called "Resource-Based Learning: A Shift in the Roles of Teacher, Lerner" which appeared in the *NASSP Bulletin* of May, 1991. Bonnie's summary was printed in the *CMLEA Newsletter*, November, 1991.
2. Moll, Luis, "Bilingual Classroom Students and Community Analysis: Some Recent Trends," *Educational Researcher*, March, 1992, p. 22.
3. *Ibid.*, p. 21-22.
4. Chart from: Moll, Luis, et al, *Community Knowledge and Classroom Practice: Combining Resources for Literacy Instruction*, Arizona, University College of Education, 1990, p. 84 (ERIC: ED 341968)
5. *Ibid.*
6. *Ibid.*
7. American Association of School Librarians and Association for Educational Communications and Technology, *Information Power*, American Library Association, 1988, p. 1.
8. *With History-Social Science for All*, California Department of Education, 1992, p. 60.
9. Yokota, Junko "Issues in Selecting Multicultural Children's Literature," *Language Arts*, March 1993, p. 159-60.
10. *With History-Social Science for All*, California Department of Education, 1992, p. 50-51.
11. *Getting the Picture*, Los Angeles County Office of Education/RETAC, 1994, p. 3:1-2.
12. Summers, Sue Lockwood, *Media Alert!: 200 Activities to Create Media-Savvy Kids*, Castle Rock, CO: Hi Willow Research & Publishing, 1997.

Chapter 6

The Instructional Process Strategies for Developing Information Literacy

Strategy 1: Writing/Keeping a Journal
Strategy 2: Challenging Learners as They Develop Questions and Pose Problems.
Strategy 3: Tapping Prior Knowledge
Strategy 4: Building Background
Strategy 5: Using Graphic Organizers
Strategy 6: Guiding Students Into, Through, and Beyond Learning Resources
Strategy 7: Developing Effective Searches
Strategy 8: I-Search: Personalizing a Research Project/Paper
Strategy 9: Establishing Audience
Strategy 10: Collaborative Grouping/Cooperative Learning
Strategy 11: Tapping the Multiple Intelligences
Strategy 12: Specially Designed Academic Instruction in English (SDAIE)

Developing Critical Thinking

Information literacy is best developed through thinking strategies. Thus library media specialists concentrate on helping students internalize a model that will stimulate thinking. In a thinking, meaning-centered curriculum, these strategies are embedded in instruction in all curricular areas rather than being taught to the student as if they were a discrete part of the curriculum. Thus, information literacy is not one of "the 4 Rs," but an integral part of them.

A common thread of many state and national documents advocating educational reform is their reference to instructional strategies that lead students to think more deeply and to unlock meaning through learning experiences. Although the curricular areas to which these learning experiences apply are varied and apparently distinct (e.g., science, ESL, foreign language, English-language arts, history-social science), the instructional strategies are strikingly similar. For example, logs or journals are recommended to help students reflect on their readings, observations or activities. Quickwrites and brainstorming are used to reveal what students already know about a question, topic, or problem. These strategies are also suitable for developing information literacy. Curriculum implementation and information literacy are integrally entwined.

Strategies to facilitate information literacy can be developed by using the best pedagogy from all areas of educational theory and practice. This chapter provides a description of some of these strategies and suggests how they can be used to achieve the objectives of both the curricular content area and information literacy.

The curricular planning team will want to adapt the strategies to the appropriate developmental level and sophistication of the students. In addition the team should evaluate the strategies carefully for the effect on student motivation and learning. Finally, the team should choose those instructional strategies that contribute to each student's ability to:
- access information,
- evaluate information, and
- use information.

Summary of Strategies

Twelve strategies have been selected for this handbook.

Strategy 1: Writing/Keeping a Journal
Strategy 2: Challenging Learners as They Develop Questions and Pose Problems.
Strategy 3: Tapping Prior Knowledge
Strategy 4: Building Background
Strategy 5: Using Graphic Organizers

Strategy 6: Guiding Students Into, Through, and Beyond Learning Resources
Strategy 7: Developing Effective Searches
Strategy 8: I-Search: Personalizing a Research Project/Paper
Strategy 9: Establishing Audience
Strategy 10: Collaborative Grouping/Cooperative Learning
Strategy 11: Tapping the Multiple Intelligences
Strategy 12: Specially Designed Academic Instruction in English (SDAIE)

As you read the following pages, think about all of your students and each of their individual language needs, their information literacy needs, and your curriculum. Then use the Instructional Planning Matrix at the end of the chapter as a framework to design possible approaches for your classroom. In addition, Appendix B provides an information literacy planning guide covering the search process competencies introduced in Chapter 3.

Strategy 1: Writing/Keeping a Journal

A log or journal is the searcher's ongoing written account of the search process. Students who are information literate must develop the ability to recognize what they are doing, analyze the results, and consider or reflect on how any learning based on these results might be applied in another situation. If learning is to take place, such reflection is essential.

Journal writing is one strategy that engages the writer in reflection. Journal writing provides unique opportunities for reflection and for the use of language allowing a flexibility that can unlock meaning and enhance understanding. Since journals are not graded or corrected they are also safe places for English learners to experiment with language.

Journals written in any language or combination of languages, enable learners to reflect, bring clarity to their thinking, and learn from their experiences. Preliterate students at any level might dictate to an aide, a tutor, a friend, or family member. The use of a simple word processor may stimulate, facilitate, and enrich journal writing.

The search process journal is used by the searcher to record the progress of a search, such as: What was my question? What did I do? What did I find? What did I learn? How did I feel? The journal also is used to project, such as: How might this experience apply to future searches? What allowed me to gain the most from this experience? What would I do differently if I had time to return to the project? In this way the journal becomes a tool for evaluating the information, the search process, and the learning that took place.

The journal format is simple. A blank sheet of paper may be divided into columns, with a heading for each column to help organize the writer's comments. The headings vary with the objective for keeping the journal. The California Literature Project identifies several different kinds of journals, most of which would be useful to students for clarifying what is happening as they access information:

- **Learning Log**: Note-taking/Note-making.
- **Problem Solution**: Problem(s)/Resolving the problem(s).
- **Reflective**: What happened/How I felt/What I learned OR What I did/What I learned/What questions do I still have?
- **Prediction/Speculation**: What happened/What might or should happen?
- **Synthesis**: What I did/What I learned/How I can use it?
- **Dialectic/Dialogue**: Quotation/Response.

The following quote from *Practical Ideas for Teaching Writing as a Process*[1] confirms the use of the journal as a tool for personal reflection.

▼ ...The self as audience is crucial to young writers' development, because it allows students to discover how the act of writing can be functional for them...Keeping logs or journals of reactions to class, events, to books or films or TV programs, and to chapters in a textbook can be a valuable first step in making personal sense of new information. Writing to work out new ideas, to raise questions, and to find out what one understands enables students to see that writing can be of direct benefit to them... Because students have an extended record of their own emerging opinions and understandings, they have themselves as resources when it comes to developing and shaping an essay or a final report. The teacher can encourage this type of writing by providing models of subject matter journals or logs, by setting aside class time for this writing, by allowing credit toward the final grade for completion of such writing, and by allowing students to keep their logs handy during the writing of tests or essays in class.

For English learners, the journal provides another means to blend both familiar and new personal experiences, knowledge, feelings, and data to create new insights. It also verifies once again the value of their own writing — in whatever language they choose to write. A sample of a generic journal page is followed by an example of a science journal.[2]

Chapter 6 • Developing Information Literacy ▼

SCIENCE JOURNAL

Observations/Facts

Suggestions: What is happening? What words describe the event? What do I see? What changes are occurring? What properties does it have?

Primary: What I know.

Hypotheses/Opinions/Questions

Suggestions: Why do I think this is happening? What questions are raised in my mind? What have I observed in the past that is similar?

Primary: What I learned.

Information Literacy

▼ Chapter 6 • Developing Information Literacy

Research Process Journal

Curricular Theme/Issue/Problem

Searcher's Thinking: My Questions	Research Process: What I Did	What I Found	What I Learned/ How I Felt

76

Information Literacy

Strategy 2: Challenging Learners as They Develop Questions and Pose Problems

Information literacy is developed in a meaningful quest for information. All components of the information literacy model (See Chapter 2) are initiated by the learner's need to know. The search for information becomes compelling when the question or problem is relevant and significant to the searcher. Typically, the most interesting and most important questions are those for which there is no single right answer, or perhaps, no clearly right answer at all.

Students ask and answer questions in all languages. In working with students, we must validate the importance of the questions that *they* are asking. We must listen carefully to *their* needs for information. It is important to acknowledge that their questions and information needs may be different from those imposed by the curriculum; yet the relevance of these personal information needs to the learner can present valuable opportunities for the development of information literacy. How can we develop these opportunities? How should we respond to students' questions?

Deborah Short, in her monograph titled *Integrating Language and Content Instruction: Strategies and Techniques* focuses on the needs of English learners and advises teachers to "increase the percentage of inferential and higher-order thinking questions asked"[3] and to "use inquiry learning,"[4] She explains that:

> These questions encourage students to expand their reasoning ability by developing and practicing skills such as hypothesizing, inferencing, analyzing, justifying, and predicting. The language used by the teacher or students need not be complex for thinking skills to be exercised. For example, to help students predict, a teacher might read the title of a story and ask, "What will this story tell us?" Teachers need to model critical thinking skills in a step-by-step approach to reasoning.[5]

In an article titled "Answering Questions and Questioning Answers, Guiding Children to Intellectual Excellence," Robert Sternberg notes that "Children are natural question-askers;" but he also identifies a critical role for adults in getting them to ask good questions. He identifies seven levels of adult responses to children's questions and arranges them as a model of interaction that can serve as a guide in helping children to develop thinking skills. The lower levels of response, although most common, do not appear to be very constructive:

Level 1.   Rejection of questions (e.g., "Don't ask").
Level 2.   Restatement of questions as responses (e.g., "That's how it is").
Level 3.   Admission of ignorance or presentation of information (e.g., "I don't know" or "The answer is . . .").

Chapter 6 • Developing Information Literacy

Beginning with Level 4, adults take the opportunity to involve the child in seeking information in order to answer the question.

Level 4. Encouragement to seek response through authority (e.g., "What does _____ say?").

Level 5. Consideration of alternative explanations (e.g., "It could be this or it could be that").

Level 6. Consideration of explanations plus means of evaluating them (e.g., "That sounds logical, but how could we check to be sure?").

Level 7. Consideration of explanations plus means of evaluating them and follow-through on evaluations (e.g., "I think you're right, but here's an almanac so let's check the index and look it up").[6]

Sternberg also notes that "as we move up the levels . . . we go from no learning to passive rote learning to analytic and creative learning. . . ." He continues:

▼ Children are taught that information can be sought out. If the parent or teacher takes responsibility for looking up the answer, children will learn that information can be sought but that someone else should do the seeking. . . . If children are offered the opportunity to find the information themselves . . . they assume the responsibility for their own learning. . . . They develop their own information-seeking skills. . . .[7]

Finally, Sternberg emphasizes that "higher-level strategies described here are ones that can be used by teachers in any classroom and by parents at any economic level."[8] We would add *and in any language.* Beth Casey and Edwin Tucker, in their article on "Problem-Centered Classrooms: Creating Lifelong Learners," suggest that "The teacher's primary role . . . is to pose open-ended problems and ask open-ended questions."[9]

Teachers and students should learn to generate essential questions. On the next two pages "Scientific Thinking Processes" suggests to teachers a variety of questions that can be asked students as they proceed through an inquiry.[10] They invite learners to access, evaluate, and use information as they formulate thoughtful responses. Because they imply many modes for accessing and responding, they are particularly applicable for English learners. While they suggest science content, they can be refocused and used to stimulate thinking in other content areas.

Scientific Thinking Processes

Observing
The scientific thinking process from which fundamental patterns of the world are constructed
Teacher's statements and questions that facilitate the process of *observing*:
- "Tell us what you see."
- "What does this feel like?"
- "Give us information about its shape and size."
- "What do you hear?"
- "Point out the properties that you observe."
- "What characteristics seem to be predominant?"
- "What properties can you find?"

Communicating
The scientific thinking process that conveys idea through social interchanges
Teacher's statements and questions that facilitate the process of *communicating*:
- "What do you see?"
- "Draw a picture of what you see through the microscope."
- "Plot the data you gathered on a graph."
- "Make a histogram of the number of raisins in slices of raisin bread."
- "Write up your experiment so it can be replicated by someone else."
- "Summarize your findings and present them to the class."

Comparing
The scientific thinking process that deals with concepts of similarities and differences
Teacher's statement and questions that facilitate the process of *comparing*:
- "How are these alike?"
- "How are these different?"
- "Compare these on the basis of similarities and differences."
- "Which is larger/smaller; softer/louder; smoother/rougher; wetter/drier?"

Ordering
The scientific thinking process that deals with patterns of sequence and seriation
Teacher's statements and questions that facilitate the process of *ordering*:
- "Which came first, second, last?"
- "What is the range in the data you gathered?"
- "In what order did these events take place?"
- "Where in the order would you place these (for inserting in a range)?"
- "Give evidence of when the pattern repeats itself."

Categorizing
The scientific thinking process that deals with patterns of groups and classes
Teacher's statements and questions that facilitate the process of *classifying*:
- "On what basis would you group these objects?"
- "Put together all those that you think belong together."
- "What is another way in which these minerals can be categorized?"
- "Identify several characteristics you used to classify these rocks."
- "What grouping best reflects the evolutionary history of these animals?"

Relating
The scientific thinking process that deals with principles concerning interactions
Teacher's statements and questions that facilitate the process of *relating*:
- "What factors caused the event to take place?"
- "Explain why this is a good or inadequate experimental design."
- "State a hypothesis so that it is testable."
- "What is the relationship between the coloration of an animal, its environment, and its predators?"
- "Using this line graph, tell the relationship between distance and time."
- "Design a study to compare the evaporation rates of different liquids (e.g., alcohol and water)."

Inferring
The scientific thinking process that deals with ideas that are remote in time and space
Teacher's statements and questions that facilitate the process of *inferring*:
- "What can you infer from these data?"
- "What arguments can you give to support your prediction?"
- "Explain how we know about quasars."
- "Under what conditions are we able to extrapolate or interpolate from data?"
- "How would you determine how many frogs live in a pond?"

Applying
The scientific thinking process by which we use knowledge
Teacher's statements and questions that facilitate the process of *applying*:
- "See who can invent a glider that will stay aloft the longest time."
- "Design a way to keep an ice cube on your desk all day without melting."
- "What political points of view must be considered if we are to protect the migration flight paths of birds over several countries?"
- "What factors must be weighed if experimentation on animals is to take place?"
- "How did different lines of evidence confirm a theory of continental drift?"[11]

Strategy 3: Tapping Prior Knowledge

For students to be engaged in meaningful problem solving or information quests, they must begin with and eventually connect to their own prior knowledge about the question or problem. The focus on prior knowledge is both a validation and confirmation of the value of their personal experience and the key to a rich source of information.

Prior knowledge is key to the academic success of all students. Alfredo Schifini emphasizes the importance of prior knowledge in the education of English learners.

> ▼ Prior knowledge — what he or she already knows, understands, believes about the world and how it operates — seems to be the single most important indicator of academic success for English learners. Concept development and comprehension both depend and build upon a student's prior knowledge.[12]

Students come from homes filled with a variety of information. Tapping into rich information that exists in each home is a strategy that validates home knowledge. Luis Moll points out that this variety of knowledge should be recognized in all families.

> ▼ ...Contrary to the deficit view about the experiences, resources, and knowledge of bilingual students, their homes, families, and communities have developed complex and rich information networks as strategies that households use to survive, to get ahead, or to thrive.[13]

Several instructional strategies are useful for tapping the prior knowledge students bring to the classroom. When engaged in these activities, students should be free to use any language or combination of languages that is most comfortable for them. Facts, details, and information that pour forth during these activities can be organized later as students begin to channel ideas. The important concept in the activities described below is the free flow of ideas. Clarifying language and checking facts for accuracy come later.

Brainstorming

Brainstorming is a basic strategy proposed for use in eliciting students' prior knowledge. When brainstorming, searchers ask, "What comes to mind when we think about this topic?" All possibilities are recorded as individual words or phrases, and all ideas are accepted. Evaluation of the ideas comes at a later stage. The purpose of brainstorming is to generate a wide range of possible approaches.

In the planning or beginning of a unit,...a non-evaluative brainstorming session or survey is conducted with the students to establish what they already know about a particular topic and to help them realize what information they don't have...The brainstorming or survey method encourages students to participate in a non-threatening activity. A lively brainstorming session can also arouse the students' natural curiosity and lead them to ask questions they might not have thought of on their own. By getting a sense of the students' prior knowledge through the brainstorming activity, the teacher can focus instruction so that it connects appropriately to the background knowledge of the students.[14]

Quickwrite

Quickwrite is a written kind of brainstorming. This description of the quickwrite activity captures the intellectual energy it generates.

> It is a special kind of writing that lets students use the act of writing itself to discover what they already know. It works only if students write without planning and without looking back...students write breathlessly/recklessly/passionately until their fingers are tired or for a given amount of time (e.g., two or three minutes). They write anything that they can think of about the topic. If students reach a point where they can't think of anything to write, they repeat the last word until something new comes to mind. Students do not worry about punctuation, spelling, or grammar...They just write![15]

K-W-L-A

K-W-L-A — These initials refer to the metacognitive format that involves a three part thinking process. Students respond to:
- What they Know,
- What they Want to know,
- What they have Learned, and
- What they feel about what they have learned (Affect).

This process activates previous knowledge, provides a purpose for investigation, and summarizes what has been learned.

Organizing Ideas

These pre-research activities can be used to help students establish the scope of research and to develop related areas of inquiry. Once ideas are generated, the searcher begins the process of organizing ideas in logical clusters to provide focus for research. Webbing and mapping ideas (discussed in detail in Strategy 5), are intermediate steps in the research process. They provide a guide to locating significant information and to outlining the final presentation.

Strategy 4: Building Background

Often, students do not have sufficient background knowledge to launch an investigation of a problem or a unit of instruction. In this case, time needs to be spent building background and the following technique could be done at any grade level.

Technique:
Students read, view, listen, and experience a wide variety of information and cultural materials on a topic in the time available.

Suggested Activities:
1. Teacher reads-aloud a book to introduce a topic.
2. Students all read and discuss the same title (fiction or non fiction) during the background phase of the unit.
3. During SSR and at home, students read or view a wide variety of titles during the background phase of the unit.
4. Students explore and consume a wide variety of audiovisual and electronic sources.
5. Teacher conducts a class discussion or seminar at the end of the background-building time. Experts add dimension to the discussion. Create a concept map with students as they draw comparisons or develop connections.

Expectations:
1. Students consume and process as much information as possible.
2. Deeper learning results as the amount of material is increased.
3. A breadth of experience stimulates a rich dialog among students.
4. As experience broadens and knowledge expands, interest and motivation increase.

Assessment Strategies:
1. Using their wide experience, students summarize what they have learned in one or more formats.
2. Teacher makes judgments of the level of student understanding.
3. Tests measure the breadth of knowledge.

Information Literacy Strategies:
1. Students become avid readers, viewers, and listeners.
2. Students recognize a need for more information.
3. Students begin to think critically about what they read, view, and hear.
4. Students begin to use a wide variety of materials upon which to draw conclusions and synthesize their ideas.

Information Literacy

5. Students start linking what they already know with a variety of new information sources.
6. Students begin the process of communicating their ideas to others.[16]

Strategy 5: Using Graphic Organizers

One of the key competencies of information literacy is the ability to organize information, thoughts, and ideas. A graphic organizer combines abstract thoughts, words, and text in a visual format that shows relationships.

The use of graphic organizers can have special benefits for English learners. Because the organizer is a visual structure, it communicates beyond specific language. Visuals take the place of prepositions and other abstract connectors. Labels are used to organize assorted bits and pieces of data, observations, and information into categories that show likeness, difference, sequence, or other relationships.

Words used in organizers may come from any language. In a language that is less familiar, words visually clustered may lead students to understandings and *a-ha's* that would otherwise be more remote. Pictures or symbols can also be used instead of words to connote facts or ideas.

Timelines are an especially effective organizer for English learners. They can create a visual timeline of any topic from "My Day" to "My Life" to "My Country's History" by drawing or clipping or copying illustrations. The text can be in any language and as comprehensive or minimal as the student chooses.

The examples on the following pages show how graphic organizers might be applied to information from scientific observation and how webbing can extend vocabulary and build verbal relationships in any language. There also are examples of the Venn diagram, a graphic organizer that is particularly applicable to Boolean logic. This important concept is applied to search strategies for many technology-based information sources.

Webbing

Webbing is a visual way of organizing related words and ideas. A web has three organizing elements: (1) main topic, (2) categories, and (3) examples.[17]

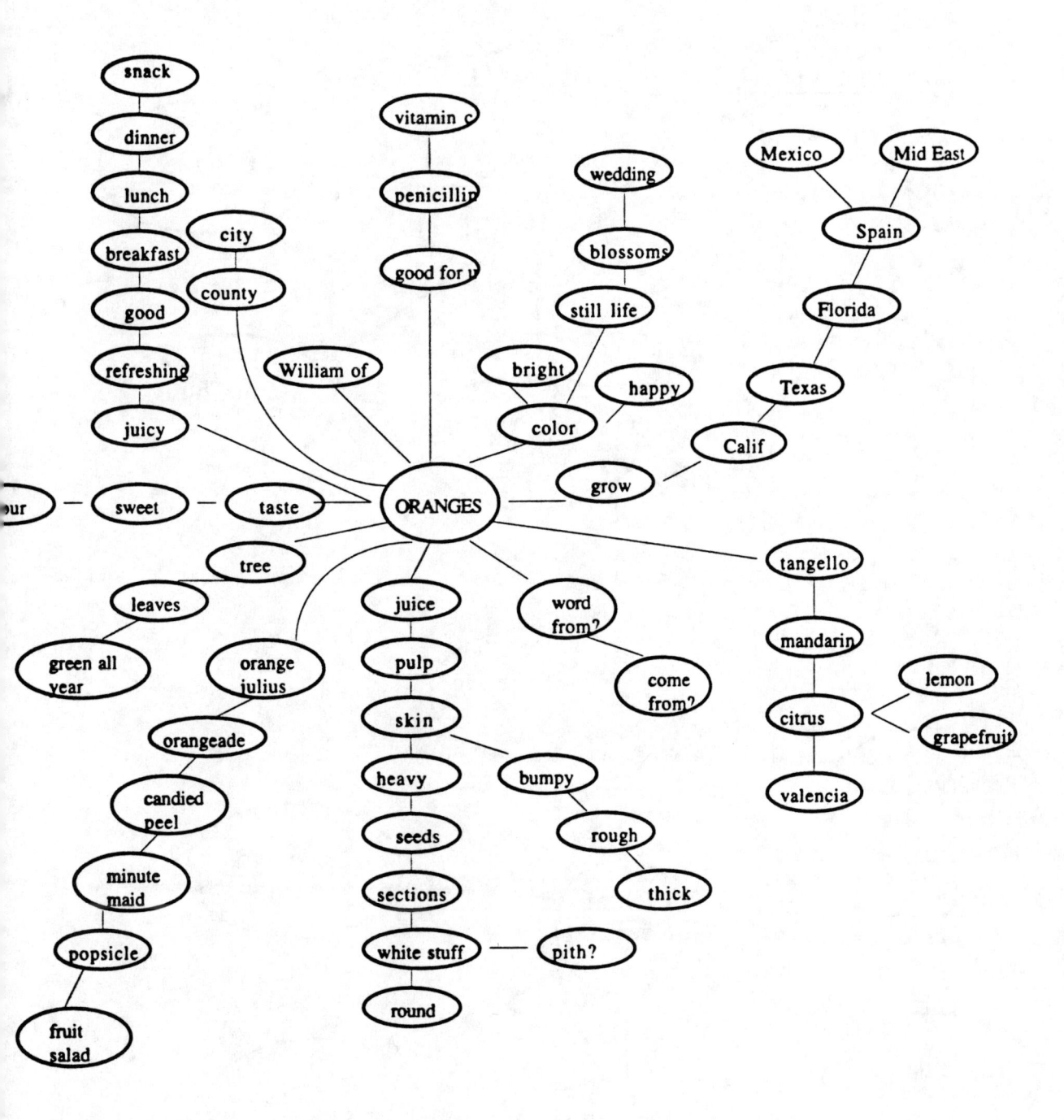

▼ Chapter 6 • Developing Information Literacy

Students can build webs in any language. The ones below were created by fourth graders in Mary Tran's class at Willmore School in the Westminster School District.[18]

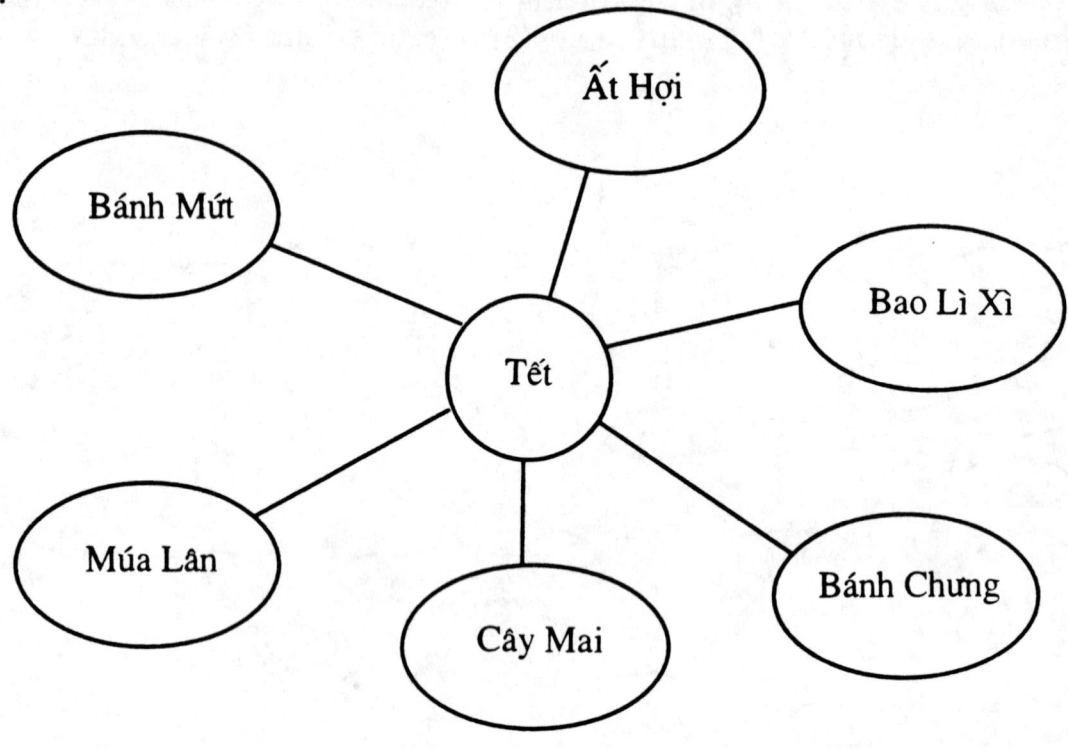

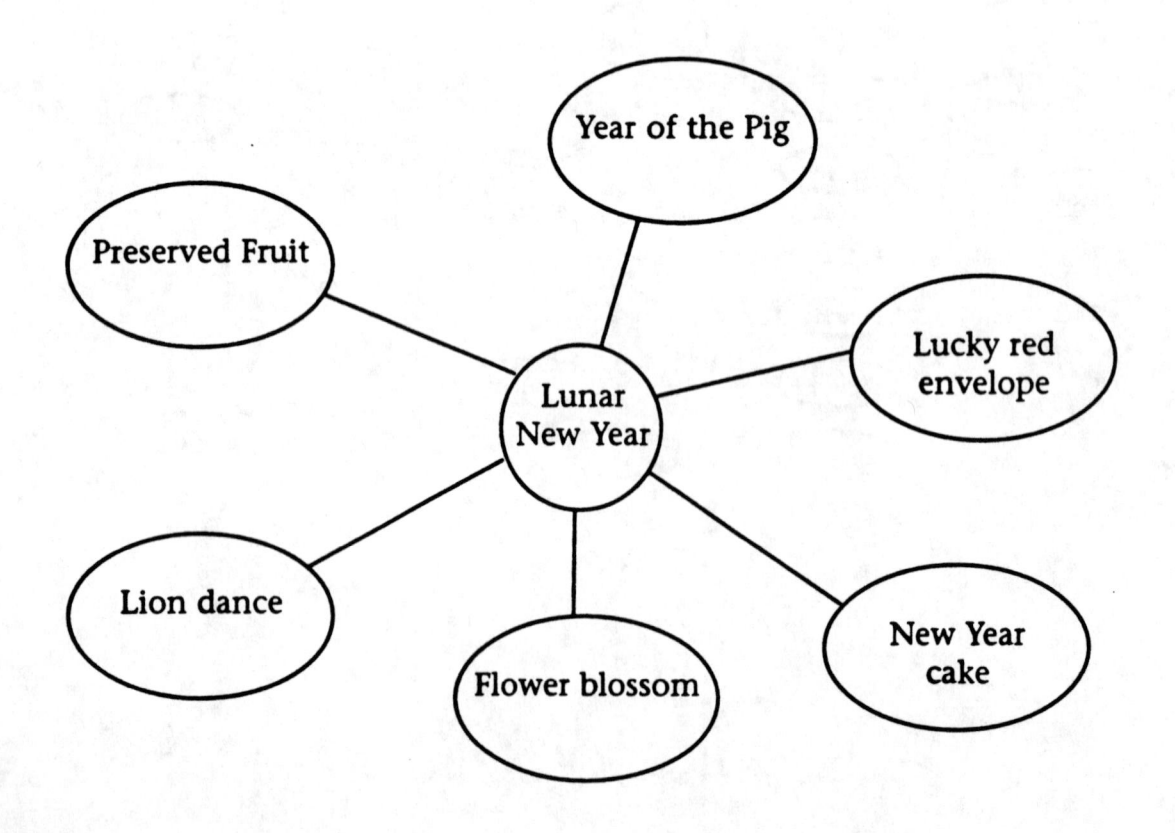

Tết web:
- Ất Hợi
- Bánh Mứt
- Bao Lì Xì
- Múa Lân
- Cây Mai
- Bánh Chưng

Lunar New Year web:
- Year of the Pig
- Preserved Fruit
- Lucky red envelope
- Lion dance
- Flower blossom
- New Year cake

Mapping

Learners create an organized visual presentation that connects ideas and shows their relationship to a main concept. Teachers may also provide a mapped lecturette for students to take notes on during a video, demonstration or text reading.[19]

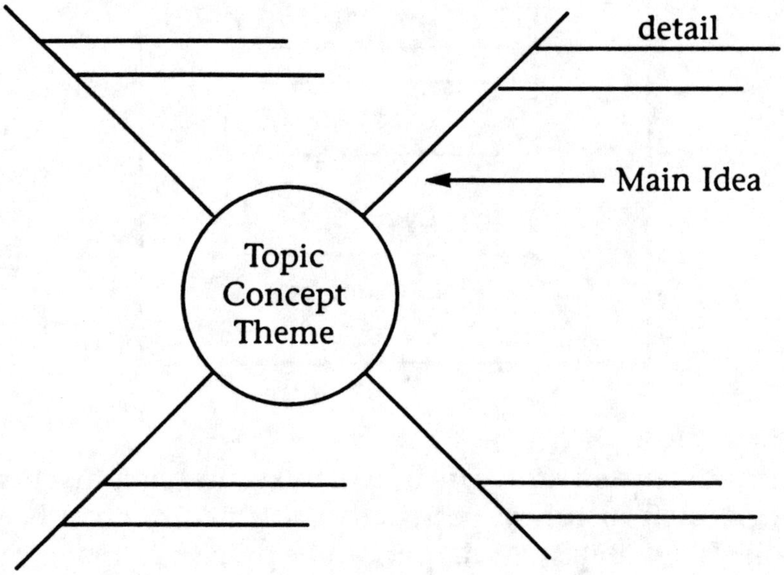
detail
Main Idea
Topic
Concept
Theme

Example of "Spider Web" Mapping

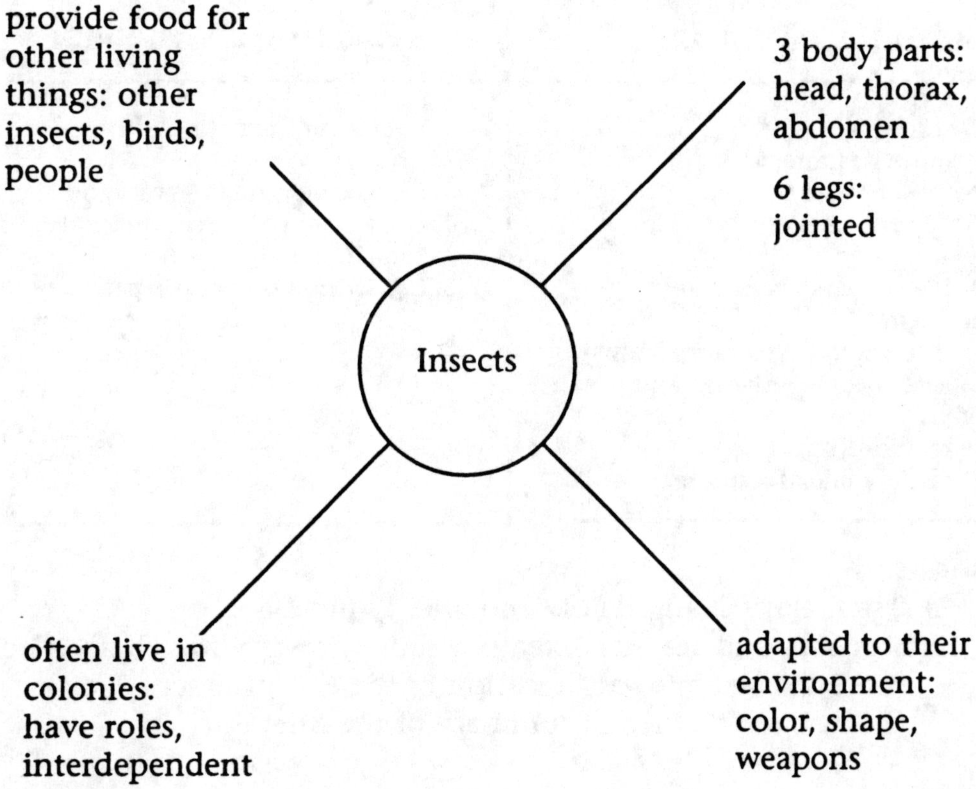
provide food for other living things: other insects, birds, people
3 body parts: head, thorax, abdomen
6 legs: jointed
Insects
often live in colonies: have roles, interdependent
adapted to their environment: color, shape, weapons

Series of Events Chain

Students may use this visual organizer to describe: (1) the stages of a cycle, (2) the steps in a linear procedure, and (3) a sequence of events.[20]

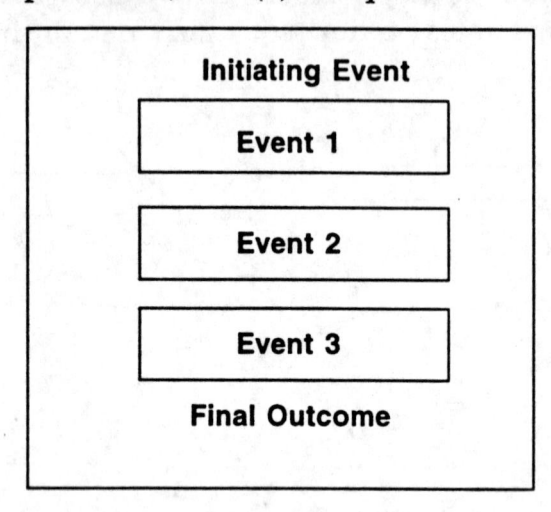

```
        Initiating Event
       ┌──────────────┐
       │   Event 1    │
       └──────────────┘

       ┌──────────────┐
       │   Event 2    │
       └──────────────┘

       ┌──────────────┐
       │   Event 3    │
       └──────────────┘
         Final Outcome
```

Time Lines

Time lines help to create a structure in which events, circumstances, or ideas can be visualized in their historical perspectives. Time lines can be made with pictures, symbols, labels, or anything that can be used to display time — and in any language. Timelines can show periods of growth and decline, relationships, and cause and effects. The following might be used as a generic student group task sheet for reading and creating time lines.[21]

Reading a Time Line	Creating a Time Line

1. Study the title.
2. Determine its framework.
  a. Note the years covered.
  b. Study the intervals between periods of time.
  c. Make space between dates the same.
3. Study the key events and mentally associate people, places, and other events.
4. Note relationships.
5. Use the time line as a summary.
	1. Decide on the period of time.
	2. Create a title.
	3. Determine time intervals and events.
	4. Use a ruler to create a proportional time line.
	5. Use written or visual labels.

*Suggestions:
1. Use literary examples of time lines as models.
2. Students and teachers create a rubric for grading that reflects the processes taken toward creation of the end product.
3. Create a short, written summary of the time line.

Comparing and Contrasting

To encourage students to compare and contrast ideas or objects, have the students make a "T" chart on a piece of butcher paper. The students first find similarities and list those on the left side of the T. Then students look for differences and list those on the right side of the T. Students display other charts and discuss them with members of the other groups.[22]

T-Chart

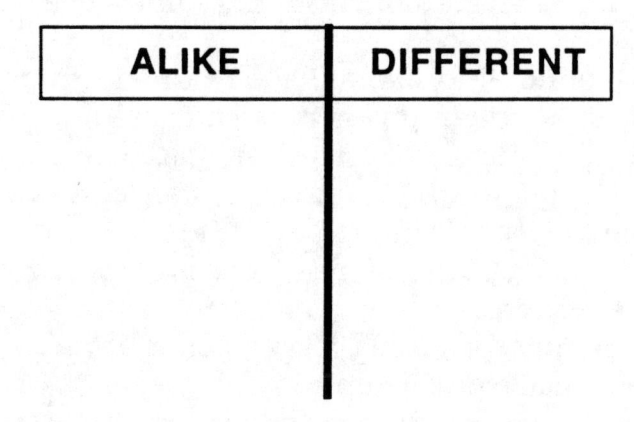

ALIKE	DIFFERENT

Venn Diagram

Using two overlapping circles, students chart the differences and similarities between two events or phenomena. A Venn diagram is also a useful visual representation of the Boolean logic that is often used for searching information in technology-based resources.

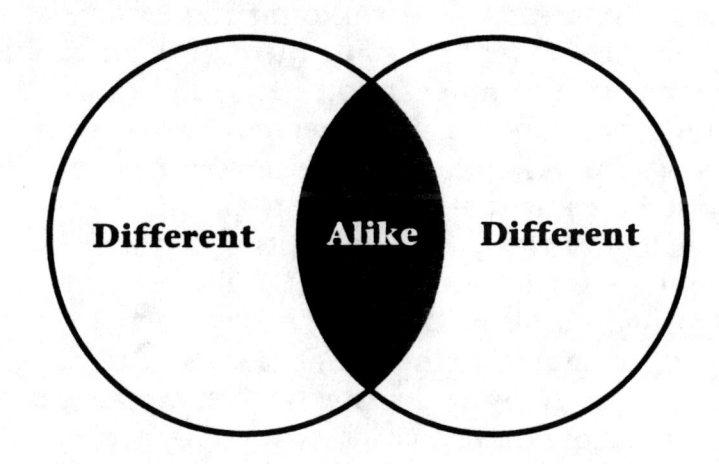

Strategy 6: Guiding Students Into, Through, and Beyond Learning Resources

"Making meaning" is an essential skill for all learners – one that can be developed as we guide students into, through, and beyond a wide variety of learning resources. For English learners this technique can be an especially important one that helps to develop comprehension and vocabulary.[23]

INTO

Build background and activate students' prior knowledge:

1. Share background information about the learning resource being introduced: topic, question or problem posed, setting, time period, author and title, country of origin, language used, and other facts.
2. Discuss general questions related to key concepts.
3. Use new vocabulary in context.
4. When bilingual versions of resources are used, discuss differences between the versions.
5. Introduce key concepts, using related books or media.
6. Have students make predictions.
7. Set purposes for the activities to follow.

THROUGH

Experience a book, video, film, or other learning resource:

1. Pair or group students for reading, listening, or viewing. When appropriate, pair English learners with fluent English speakers.
2. Have students re-predict as new information is added.
3. Think aloud with students to guide them through confusing parts.
4. Check for language comprehension frequently.
5. Read or review quickly to get an overview of the content (skimming).
6. Make analogies to link prior knowledge with new knowledge.
7. Compare audio and visual information to text:
    a. If the medium is text, have students use visual or audio means to communicate their understandings of the content.
    b. If the medium is visual or audio, have students use oral or written means to communicate their understandings of the content.
8. Have students use nonverbal strategies to summarize concepts.
9. Ask open-ended questions that have no right or wrong answers.
10. Have students use mapping or organizing strategies to clarify comprehension.

BEYOND

Extend students' learning:

1. Discuss INTO questions in light of students' experience with the learning resource used.
2. Engage students in activities that help them to connect the new information to their personal experience and tie new vocabulary to prior knowledge.
3. Discuss questions such as "What if? Why?"
4. Engage students in activities that relate the learning resource to other curricular areas.
5. Compare resources that deal with similar themes and issues.
6. Explore related resources (e.g., on the same topic, in the same genre, by the same author or illustrator, with a similar plot structure or similar character(s), or in other media, language, or format).

Strategy 7: Developing Effective Searches

One of the most challenging aspects of the search process is the analysis of the problem and the related need for information. What is it I really need to know? How is this kind of information likely to be organized or identified? What headings, key words, descriptions can I use? How are parts of this topic/problem related to each other? As students work out these problems, they are developing search strategies. As new technology provides access to exponentially increasing amounts and varieties of data, our ability to retrieve the needed information will depend on the extent to which effective search strategies can be analyzed and developed.

The following section presents two basic search strategy concepts: 1) key word search, and 2) Boolean logic. While these are sophisticated intellectual concepts, they should be introduced early and developed in depth consistent with students' intellectual development. These strategies can be applied to searching for information in any format, from library catalogs to Internet sources.

▼ Chapter 6 • Developing Information Literacy

Key Word Search

Students need to develop skills in analyzing the key concepts and elements in their search questions to develop appropriate search strategies. How is information on their topic likely to be indexed? What key words or phrases will they need to use? The following materials suggest questions that should help students develop patterns for exploring their information needs. While these basic patterns can be applied in most situations, they are only examples of search analysis concepts. You and your students may discover or develop other patterns that can be used in developing search strategies.[24]

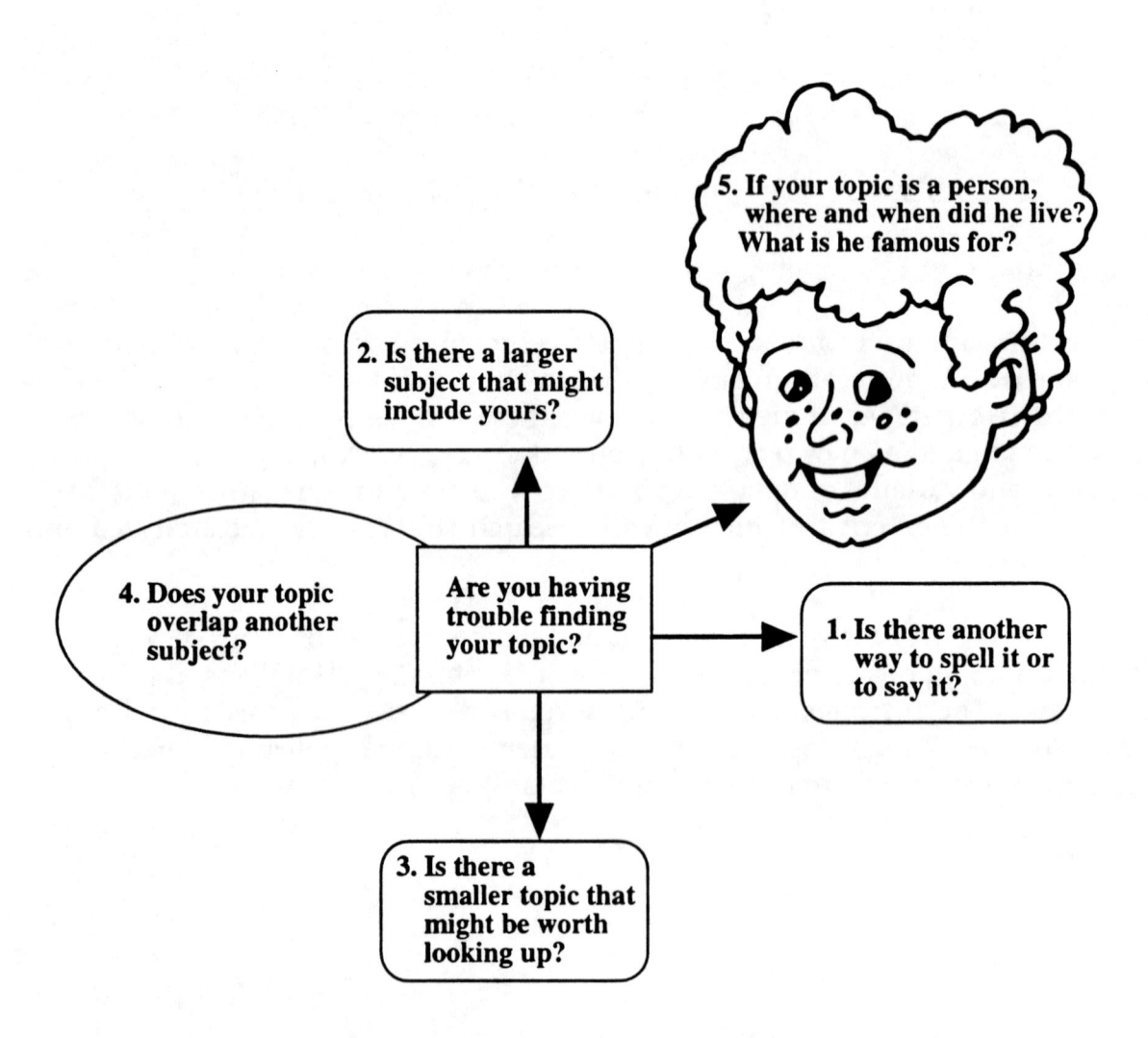

Are you having trouble finding your topic?

1. Is there another way to spell it or to say it?
2. Is there a larger subject that might include yours?
3. Is there a smaller topic that might be worth looking up?
4. Does your topic overlap another subject?
5. If your topic is a person, where and when did he live? What is he famous for?

MY SEARCH

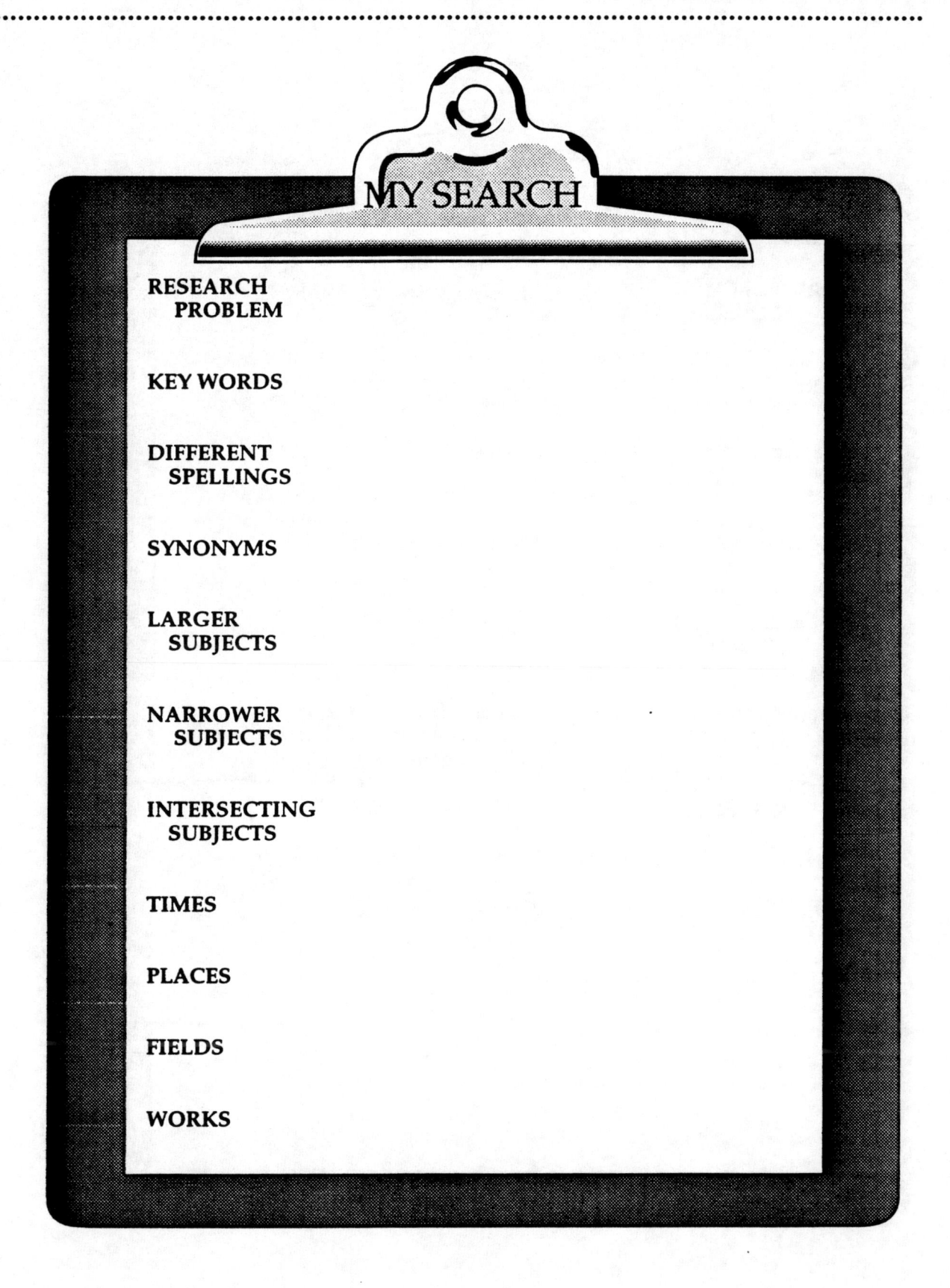

RESEARCH PROBLEM

KEY WORDS

DIFFERENT SPELLINGS

SYNONYMS

LARGER SUBJECTS

NARROWER SUBJECTS

INTERSECTING SUBJECTS

TIMES

PLACES

FIELDS

WORKS

MY SEARCH

RESEARCH PROBLEM	*How do you raise butterflies?*
KEY WORDS	Butterflies, Caterpillars Moths, Butterfly farming
DIFFERENT SPELLINGS	Butterfly
SYNONYMS	Butterfly attracting Butterfly gardening
LARGER SUBJECTS	Insects, Lepidoptera Insect rearing Entomology
NARROWER SUBJECTS	Names of different species: Monarch butterfly, Milkweed butterfly, Viceroy butterfly, etc.
INTERSECTING SUBJECTS	Butterflies, Conservation Ecology

MY SEARCH

RESEARCH PROBLEM	*How were the Japanese Americans who were placed in relocation camps in the United States during World War II treated?*
KEY WORDS	Japanese Americans, Relocation camps
DIFFERENT SPELLINGS	
SYNONYMS	Nisei, Internment camps
LARGER SUBJECTS	World War, 1939-1945 Prisoners of War -- United States Concentration camps, Refugees Evacuation of civilians
NARROWER SUBJECTS	Manzanar, Tule Lake Relocation Center (other individual relocation camps) Koremaster v. United States
INTERSECTING SUBJECTS	WorldWar, 1939-1945--Japanese Americans United States, Internment

Boolean Logic

For many kinds of information searches it is important to analyze and develop relationships between the concepts or key ideas that you are using. This is especially important in computer-assisted searching, either online or on CD-ROM. Once you have identified concepts and selected suitable key words or phrases, you can establish the relationships that most clearly define or limit your search. For most electronic searching three words - *or, and, not* - are used as logical operators in a system developed by George Boole, a mathematician. The basic uses of these Boolean operators are defined briefly below. The diagrams used to illustrate these logical operators are called Venn diagrams.[25]

Search question: How are German Shepherds trained to be seeing eye dogs?

Or
Used for synonymous terms; indicates that you want information on either topic.
Example:
    Seeing Eye dogs
        or
    Guide dogs

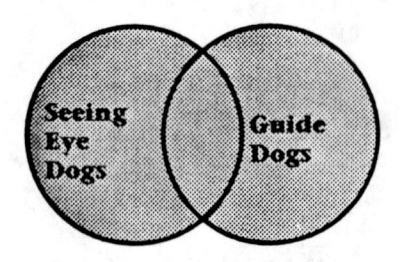

You get lots of information.

And
Used to connect two terms or ideas; you want only the information that contains both concepts together.
Example:
    Seeing Eye dogs
        and
    German Shepherds

Information is limited

Not
Used to exclude a term or idea; you do not want information on this topic.
Example:
    Seeing Eye dogs
        not
    Golden Retrievers

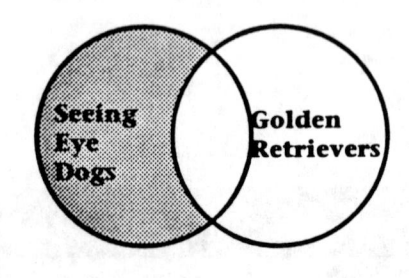

Information is narrowed

Strategy 8: I-Search: Personalizing a Research Project/Paper

Ken Macrorie has coined the term "I-Search" to connote an original search to fulfill the searcher's need for information. Students learn and practice searching skills: gathering information, sifting it, analyzing and synthesizing it, and then reformulating it for an important purpose of their own. In his classes, students compose a paper chronicling their search and what they found.

Any search can become an I-Search if the student takes ownership of the question, problem or topic. The following steps can be applied to the development of any paper or of any other kind of presentation that is a product of research.

Steps in an I-Search Paper

Jenee Gossard, educational consultant, describes a process that she uses with students.

1. **Letting a Topic Choose You:** Macrorie asks students to "Allow something to choose you that you want intensely to know or possess .... that will fulfill a need in your life rather than a teacher's notion of what would be good for you to pursue." My students cluster, share, and discuss possible topics of personal significance. For one or two of these they write short answers to the following questions:
   a. Why is this issue important right now in your life?
   b. What do you already know about it?
   After sharing their possible topics in a small group, students focus on the topic that is most meaningful to them personally.

2. **Searching:** Students gather information on their topic in several ways:
   a. Talking: casual conversations to formal interviews.
   b. Observation: sensory data, information, impressions.
   c. Participation: first-hand experience.
   d. Collecting: brochures, fliers, manuals, ads, objects.
   e. Reading: relevant print sources.

3. **Sharing and Reporting:** Students share and report regularly on their search process:
   a. Initial sharing: students share topics in small groups (5-7), then with the whole class.
   b. Weekly updates: a two-page summary detailing the week's progress, shared orally in read-around groups.
   c. Plenary sessions: (every other week) five-minute written summaries *of major* progress to date, read aloud to the class.

▼ Chapter 6 • Developing Information Literacy

4. **Practice Assignments:** Students draft, share, and revise two short papers to practice skills needed in the I-Search paper:
   a. Observation report using all sensory information.
   b. Interview quotes, summaries, connective narration.

5. **Readable Rough Draft:** Students synthesize their I-Search material (notes, updates, collected materials, practice assignments) into a coherent record of their search (5-8 pages). Beginning the draft, groups discuss:
   a. Purpose and audience.
   b. Organizational strategies: chronological, impressionistic, flashback, topical.
   c. Development: details, examples, descriptions, anecdotes, summaries, direct quotations, paraphrases.
   d. Structure: the draft must have at least four chapters addressing:
      • What did you search for?
      • Why was it important to you?
      • What did you know about it to begin with?
      • What did you learn (or not learn)?
      • What do you plan to do next, if anything?

6. **Revising:**
   a. Students exchange rough drafts and read several silently, then share their own orally with their read-around group.
   b. After reading and hearing a number of drafts, partners exchange papers, and make written comments on various aspects of organization and development.
   c. Students revise rough drafts based on their partners' comments and other drafts they have seen.
   d. Students attach cover sheet to all revised drafts:
      • What specific changes did you make in this draft?
      • What effects do these changes create?
      • How do you feel about your paper now?

7. **Editing:** In small groups or pairs, students exchange and revise drafts pointing out effective/weak language: precise diction, fresh expressions, clichés, repetition, English, dead words, passive voice, etc. As a final step, pairs or groups proofread each other's papers for surface errors in conventions.

8. **Preparing for Presentation of I-Search Papers:** Students present their papers to the class orally, three papers per class over a period of ten days. The room is arranged theater-style and guests are invited to each day's presentation.
   a. To help students with effective titles for their I-Search projects, the following written exercise might be used in class:
      • Write a question as a working title: "Should I become a physical therapist?"
      • Write three more titles: another question, one using alliteration, one completely ridiculous.

- Cluster significant words/ ideas from your topic.
- Write three more titles using ideas from the cluster.
- Write a title reflecting the most important idea/ insight from your search.
- A decision prompted by your search.
- A bumper sticker advertising your search (6 words or less).
  b. Invitation and program sent to invited guests (other teachers, administrators, classified staff, parents, local newspapers, etc.).
  c. Oral skills practice session.

9. **Presenting the Final Draft:** Students read their I-Search papers orally, and then hand in their completed papers. The students:
   a. Complete an oral presentation response sheet: each class member completes one evaluation sheet for one speaker each day.
   b. Do self-evaluation and readers' affidavits: completed and signed forms must accompany the final draft.
   c. Complete written final drafts due the day following the oral presentations.
   d. Receive grades on the oral and the written versions of their I-Search.[26]

Strategy 9: Establishing Audience

Learners who are developing information literacy must think about the information they have gathered in order to evaluate, interpret, and make meaning. They should also have a purpose for using this information. A natural, challenging, and effective way to motivate and propel analysis and use of information is to establish an audience with which to communicate. Personalizing the communication of information adds the essential ingredient of relevance. The audience may be familiar or remote, an individual or a group, personal or official. The communication may be written (letters, reports); oral (telephone conversations, formal presentations, dramatizations); or visual (cartoons, displays, videotapes). The significance of establishing audience is that the learner has to determine the best way to communicate information to a specific person or group. The information has to be sorted, clarified, organized, reduced to essentials, or amplified with details and examples that help the reader, listener, or viewer understand the meaning.

English learners can extend the scope and impact of personal and group communication by helping their classmates reach new and important audiences. For example, they may be able to communicate effectively with individuals, groups, or agencies in the community or in other areas of the world as perhaps no one else can. When using nonverbal modes of communication, English learners can work together with their native English-speaking classmates to reach their common audiences. By offering students options to explore varied modes of communication, teachers can include English learners in integrated heterogeneous groups.

Mary Healy, Co-director of the Bay Area Writing Projects, emphasizes the importance of students' communicating with a real audience that can respond and suggests examples:

> ▼ Beyond the variations of teacher as audience, many others can profitably be addressed in classroom writing. Students can write for their peers – either fellow students in their classes or those in other classes or other schools. The key point here is that this writing be genuinely addressed to an audience that will, indeed, read and respond to the writing. Only through this genuine response, with all the attendant confusion and misunderstandings, can a real sense of audience develop.[27]

Applications to history-social science are obvious:

> ▼ Writing letters to contemporary figures, agencies, or a friend or relative about current or historical issues can help students clarify their thinking on a topic and improve their basic writing skills. Fourth-grade students may write a letter to Cesar Chavez, expressing their views on pesticides used on the farms in the San Joaquin Valley. Students in grade twelve may write letters to the editor of a newspaper or to governmental officials or agencies regarding contemporary issues, such as acid rain, health care, taxes, or the plight of homeless people. Students may find it easier to express themselves about an issue in a letter format in which they use their own words and style than in an essay format. Students may give examples of, and elaborate on, what they relate to personally when they do not have to write "for the teacher." This activity can encourage students to think critically about their opinions and about what they have learned. They will have to judge the information they have gathered and draw conclusions based on solid evidence.[28]

Strategy 10: Collaborative Grouping/Cooperative Learning

So much has been said in recent years about collaboration and cooperation for learning that the benefits seem obvious. For most of us experiences with collaboration clearly demonstrate that the collective pooling and interplay of information, perspectives, and insights can result in greater and more significant learning. The product of the whole group is typically greater than the sum of its parts. There is value added for everyone.

Attributes and characteristics of cooperative learning are excerpted from several sources.

- Cooperative learning . . . provides for diversity and individuality in learning styles and aids students in the socialization process. Paired and group activities promote student interaction and decrease the anxiety many students feel when they must perform alone for the teacher in front of the class. It is important for each student in the group to have a task which he or she may accomplish and thus contribute to the activity (e.g., by being recorder, final copy scribe, illustrator, materials collector, reporter). The ideal size for these groups ranges from 2 to 5 students. Special consideration should be given to students whose home culture may make them feel uncomfortable participating in cooperative learning activities. While all students should be invited to participate, the teacher should respect the wishes of any student who prefers not to participate.[29]

- Cooperative learning in group situations [can] minimize unproductive competition and the isolation of individuals. . . .Working together in activities not only promotes learning in history-social science but also enhances the acquisition of language and strengthens participatory skills.[30]

- Bilingual students can be encouraged to meet and review, share and discuss understandings in their primary languages when helpful. Students benefit from developing their note-taking skills and from discussing, in small groups, what they understood from the information presented to the class.[31]

- Information gap . . . activities, which include jigsaws, problem-solving, and simulations, are set up so each student (in a class, or more generally, in a group) has one or two pieces of information needed to solve the puzzle but not all the necessary information. Students must work together, sharing information while practicing their language, negotiating, and critical thinking skills.[32]

- [Use] Focus Trios. Before a video, lecture, or reading, divide students into groups of three and have students summarize together what they already know about the subject and generate questions they may have. Afterwards, the trios answer questions, discuss new information, and formulate new questions.[33]

- [In] Problem Solvers [each group has a] problem to solve. Each student in the group must contribute to part of the solution. Groups can decide who does what, but they must show how all members contributed. Alternatively, they can reach a decision or solution together, but each must be able independently to explain how to solve the problem.[35]

- In a jigsaw activity, each person reads and studies part of a selection, then teaches what he or she has learned to the other members of the group. Each then quizzes the group members until satisfied that everyone knows his or her part thoroughly.[34]

The following jigsaw activity is an example of a cooperative experience that could be created at almost any grade level or topical area.

Jigsaw[36]

Technique:
A topic is assigned by the teacher and divided into pieces or parts among individual students or groups. Students share and bring the pieces together.

Suggested Activities:

1. Teachers (students can help) create the engaging problem.
2. Students use the research process to explore their assigned part.
3. Students report back to their group to share and extend their knowledge.
4. Entire group participates in a culminating experience to discern patterns and trends across the pieces.
5. As a whole group, students communicate and present their knowledge as an exhibition, a written paper, a video, a multimedia project, a science fair project, a history-day project, a world wide web page, etc.

Expectations:

1. Students working on an engaging problem are interested learners.
2. Students learn to work effectively as a group in a facilitated learning environment.
3. Peer groups develop social skills and behaviors.
4. Students build self esteem and become empowered as they share in groups.

5. Students become responsible for teaching information to others
6. Students realize that the whole is greater than the sum of its parts.

Assessment Strategies:

1. Quality is more important than quantity or glitz.
2. Students are on task as the project develops.
3. Students communicate effectively in the chosen format.
4. Knowledge is applied to real world problems.
5. The culminating activity creates a complete picture of the puzzle.
6. Students excel on content-based tests.

Information Literacy Strategies:

1. Students focus on the problem within their assigned topic.
2. Students recognize a need for more information and are able to locate a wide variety of appropriate and applicable resources.
3. Students think critically about what they read, view, and hear.
4. Students use a wide variety of information to draw conclusions and synthesis of their ideas.
5. Students link what they already know with a variety of new information sources.
6. Students communicate their ideas to others in a way that contributes to the whole.

Strategy 11: Tapping the Multiple Intelligences

Student learning styles should influence the types of resources used and the final presentation of the synthesized information. Howard Gardener has identified seven intelligences, which in combination affect an individual's thinking and learning styles. David Lazear has assembled a Multiple Intelligences Toolbox of creative strategies. Any of these strategies might be used to engage learners in developing information literacy.[37]

VERBAL/LINGUISTIC
- Reading
- Vocabulary
- Formal Speech
- Journal/Diary Keeping
- Creative Writing
- Poetry
- Verbal Debate
- Impromptu Speaking
- Humor/Jokes
- Storytelling

LOGICAL/MATHEMATICAL
- Abstract Symbols/Formulas
- Outlining
- Graphic Organizers
- Number Sequences
- Calculation
- Deciphering Codes
- Forcing Relationships
- Syllogisms
- Problem Solving
- Pattern Games

VISUAL/SPATIAL
- Guided Imagery
- Active Imagination
- Color Schemes
- Patterns/Designs
- Painting
- Drawing
- Mind-Mapping
- Pretending
- Sculpture
- Pictures

MUSICAL/RHYTHMIC
- Rhythmic Patterns
- Vocal Sounds/Tones
- Music Composition/Creation
- Percussion Vibrations
- Humming
- Environmental Sounds
- Instrumental Sounds
- Singing
- Tonal Patterns
- Music Performance

MULTIPLE INTELLIGENCES TOOLBOX

INTRAPERSONAL
- Silent Reflection Methods
- Metacognition Techniques
- Thinking Strategies
- Emotional Processing
- "Know Thyself" Procedures
- Mindfulness Practices
- Focusing/Concentrating Skills
- Higher-Order Reasoning
- Complex Guided Imagery
- "Centering" Practices

INTERPERSONAL
- Giving Feedback
- Intuiting Other's Feelings
- Cooperative Learning Strategies
- Person-to-Person Communication
- Empathy Practices
- Division of Labor
- Collaboration Skills
- Receiving Feedback
- Sensing Other's Motives
- Group Projects

BODY/KINESTHETIC
- Folk/Creative Dance
- Role Playing
- Physical Gestures
- Drama
- Martial Arts
- Body Language
- Physical Exercise
- Mime
- Inventing
- Sports Games

Strategy 12: Specially Designed Academic Instruction In English (SDAIE)

SDAIE is an abbreviation resulting from the development of new terminology and standards for instructional methodologies used with English learners. It refers to Specially Designed Academic Instruction in English and replaces the term sheltered English.

English learners have the opportunity to become information literate in both their primary language and English. Sheltered English instruction SDAIE is a combination of instructional strategies that can contribute to the development of information literacy in a student's second language. Sheltered instruction is "designed to make academically rigorous subject matter understandable to second-language speakers at intermediate fluency or above. This is usually done by teaching new concepts in context and providing additional linguistic clues. Many of the teaching techniques geared to provide comprehensible input in the second-language classroom are now being used by content teachers."[38]

Print resources can be useful in supporting English language learning if they have high readability, illustrations that are integral to the text, rich content that supports common curriculum, highlighted vocabulary, and are engaging to the reader. In the section below, Dr. Alfredo Schifini identifies the key concepts of SDAIE. When these concepts are translated into teacher and learner behaviors, they are directly applicable to the development of information literacy.

Cornerstones of Sheltered Instruction

Comprehensible Input

This is a construct first articulated by Stephen Krashen to describe understandable and meaningful language directed at people acquiring a second language. Krashen has characterized "comprehensible second language input" as language which the second language acquirer already knows (1) plus a range of new language (1+1) which is made comprehensible in formal schooling contexts by the use of certain planned strategies.

Among these strategies are: (a) focus on communicating a meaningful message rather than focus on language forms; (b) frequent use of concrete contextual referents such as visuals, props, graphics, and realia; (c) lack of restriction on the use of the primary language by the second language acquirers; (d) careful grouping practices, such as the use of cooperative learning; (e) minimal overt language form correction by the teaching staff; and (f) establishment of positive and motivating learning environments.

Prior Knowledge

This seems to be the single most important indicator of academic success for language minority students. Concept development and comprehension both depend and build upon a student's prior knowledge: what he or she already knows, understands, and believes about the world and how it operates. Determining the extent and nature of a student's prior knowledge is essential for a teacher because if a student does not possess the appropriate knowledge required for a particular lesson or activity, he or she will not be able to succeed at that lesson or activity. Once we know what our students already know, then we can determine if a gap exists between what they know and what they need to know to undertake a specific task. If such a gap does exist, teachers must fill that gap, and provide the requisite prior knowledge so that both the teachers and students can then build on that critical foundation. A note of caution: prior knowledge is dependent on a variety of socioeconomic, cultural, and linguistic factors.

Contextualization

Based on recent empirical research, we know that it is not necessary to simplify oral or written language in order for students to understand important concepts. What is necessary is to *contextualize* that language. This means that we surround difficult or new vocabulary or grammatical structures or ideas with such things as informal definitions, repetition, paraphrasing, examples, comparisons, contrasts, extended description, synonyms, and antonyms.

The advantage of doing this as opposed to simplifying language is that when we contextualize language we still expose students to the complex and rich vocabulary and grammatical structures and ideas that we want them to eventually acquire. If we only simplify, students will never have complex structures modeled for them. Examples of contextualization in the classroom include: visual support, diagrams, charts, student center tasks, cooperative activities, manipulatives, and props.

Negotiation for Meaning

Negotiation for meaning, a key characteristic of communicative interaction, facilitates and promotes both language acquisition and cognitive development. It occurs when participants find themselves in situations where they have a vested interest in understanding messages and having their own messages understood. In these situations, where they must interact linguistically, they naturally do all sorts of things to facilitate comprehension: explain, repeat, expand, paraphrase, pause, question, etc.

In order for negotiation of meaning to occur, however, there must exist both (a) a focus on task (there is something specific to do, to accomplish): and (b) informational equality (all the participants have a need to share information, to interact, because no one participant has all the necessary information to complete the task). Rather, each participant has information that the others need if they are to accomplish their task, In a classroom, negotiation for meaning can be achieved through role planing, problem solving, activities where students create products, cooperative learning, and paired skill building.[39]

Designing the Mix for English Learners

SDAIE, as well as all other instructional strategies used with English learners must lead to:

- Academic success,
- Development of information literacy, and
- Implementation of curriculum.

Research and experience confirm what program guidelines and current curriculum documents recommend as language delivery modes that lead to success for these learners:

- English language development (ELD),
- Content area instruction in the primary language,
- Specially Designed Academic Instruction in English (SDAIE), and
- Mainstream English.

In addition, approaches that foster positive self-image and cross-cultural development should be incorporated for all students.

▼ Chapter 6 • Developing Information Literacy

Instructional Planning Checklist

How can the curricular planning team use the strategies identified in this chapter to facilitate planning? Try the following checklist as your review the planning process:

1. Review the sampling of instructional strategies covered in chapter 6:
    Strategy 1: Writing/Keeping a Journal
    Strategy 2: Challenging Learners as They Develop Questions and Pose Problems.
    Strategy 3: Tapping Prior Knowledge
    Strategy 4: Building Background
    Strategy 5: Using Graphic Organizers
    Strategy 6: Guiding Students Into, Through, and Beyond Learning Resources
    Strategy 7: Developing Effective Searches
    Strategy 8: I-Search: Personalizing a Research Project/Paper
    Strategy 9: Establishing Audience
    Strategy 10: Collaborative Grouping/Cooperative Learning
    Strategy 11: Tapping the Multiple Intelligences
    Strategy 12: Specifically Designed Academic Instruction in English (SDAIE)

2. Consider how these strategies might be used to help students:
    • Access information,
    • Evaluate information, and
    • Use/generate information.

3. Use the Instructional Planning Matrix on the following page to plot possible ways to engage all learners in your classroom and promote their information literacy while implementing curriculum and achieving desired outcomes.[40]

Information Literacy

Instructional Planning Matrix

Curricular Area _____

Language Proficiency of Learners _____

Framework Concept or Theme _____

Project/Learning Outcome _____

Strategy Mix:
In designing your curricular unit, determine and check (√) the instructional strategies you will use to help your students access, evaluate, and use or generate information. Add codes as appropriate to indicate the language delivery modes that will best support your students' needs. English Language.Development (ELD); Primary Language (PL); Specially Designed Academic Instruction in English (SDAIE); Mainstream English Instruction (MEI). Show where you will incorporate approaches that foster positive images of self and others and cross-cultural development (I/C) for all students.

Instruction Strategies	Access information	Evaluate information	Use/generate information
Writing/Keeping a journal			
Developing Questions/Posing Problems			
Tapping Prior Knowledge			
Building Background			
Using Graphic Organizers			
Guiding Students Into, Through, and Beyond Learning			
Developing Effective Searches			
I-Search: Personalizing a Research Project/Paper			
Establishing Audience			
Collaborative Grouping/Cooperative Learning			
Tapping the Multiple Intelligences			
Specifically Designed Academic Instruction in English (SDAIE)			

Information Literacy

NOTES

1. *Practical Ideas for Teaching Writing as a Process at the High School and College Levels*, California Department of Education, 1997, p.74-75.
2. The Science Journal example is from *Getting the Picture*, Los Angeles County Office of Education/RETAC, 1994, p. 3:12.
3. Short, Deborah J. *Integrating Language and Content Instruction: Strategies and Techniques*, National Clearinghouse for Bilingual Education, Program Information Guide Series, Fall 1991, p. 5
4. *Ibid.*, p. 6.
5. *Ibid.*, p. 5.
6. Sternberg, Robert "Answering Questions and Questioning Answers: Guiding Children to Intellectual Excellence," *Phi Delta Kappan,* October, 1994, pp. 136-38
7. *Ibid.*, p. 137.
8. *Ibid.*
9. Casey, Beth and Edwin Tucker, "Problem Centered Classrooms: Creating Lifelong Learners," *Phi Delta Kappan*, October, 1994, p. 140.
10. The sample thought-provoking questions of the Scientific Thinking Processes handout are taken from the *Science Framework for California Public Schools*, California Department of Education, 1990.
11. Condensed from "Science Process and the Teaching of Science" Reprinted with permission from *Science Framework for California Public Schools*, California Department of Education, 1990.
12. Schifini, Alfredo. *Getting the Picture.* Los Angeles County Office of Education/RETAC, 1994, p. 27.
13. Moll, Louis. "Bilingual Classroom Studies and Community Analysis: Some Recent Trends." *Educational Researcher*, March, 1992, p. 21.
14. *With History-Social Science for All*, California Department of Education, 1987, p. 47.
15. *Meaning-Making Strategies for a Literature-Based Curriculum*, California Literature Project, 1992.
16. Information Literacy Task Force, Region VII, California Technology Assistance Project. "Information Literacy: Guidelines for Kindergarten through Grade 12," Published on the World Wide Web of Fresno County Office of Education, Fresno, CA, 1996.
17. From *Research as a Process: Developing Skills for Life in an Information Society*, Los Angeles County Office of Education, 1989, p.10.
18. Developed by Mary Tran, submitted by Sue Crosby, Westminster School District.
19. From: *Getting the Picture*, Los Angeles County Office of Education/RETAC, 1994, p. 3:8.
20. *Getting the Picture.* Los Angeles County Office of Education/RETAC, 1994, p. 3:9.
21. Developed by Joyce Roth. Text adapted from: *The Story of America: Beginnings to 1914*, by John A. Garraty. Holt, Rinehart and Winston, Inc. 1991, p. 21.
22. From: *Getting the Picture*, Los Angeles County Office of Education/RETAC, 1994, p. 3:9.
23. Adapted from material developed by Los Angeles Unified School District Library Services.
24. The material on key word search strategies is adapted with permission of the author, Lillian Wehmeyer, from *The School Librarian as Educator.* Libraries Unlimited, 1986.
25. Adapted and reprinted with permission from *DIALOG Classmate Student Workbook*. DIALOG Information Services, Inc., 1987. All rights reserved.
26. For full development of I-Search concepts and strategies see Ken Macrorie, *The I-Search Paper*, revised edition of *Searching Writing* (Boynton/Cook, 1988).
27. *Practical Ideas for Teaching Writing as a Process at the High School and College Levels*, California Department of Education, 1997, p. 75.
28. *With History-Social Science for All*, California Department of Education, 1987, pp. 49-50.
29. Short, Deborah J., *Integrating Language and Content Instruction: Strategies and Techniques*, National Clearinghouse for Bilingual Education, Program Information Guide Series, Fall 1991, pp. 5-6.
30. *With History-Social Science for All*, California Department of Education, 1987, p. 34.
31. *Ibid.*, p. 48.

32. Short, Deborah J., *Integrating Language and Content Instruction: Strategies and* Techniques, National Clearinghouse for Bilingual Education, Program Information Guide Series, Fall 1991, p. 7.
33. *Getting the Picture*, Los Angeles County Office of Education/RETAC, 1994, p. 3:11.
34. *Ibid.*
35. *Ibid.*
36. Information Literacy Task Force, Region VII, California Technology Assistance Project. "Information Literacy Guidelines for Kindergarten Through Grade 12," Published on the World Wide Web of Fresno County Office of Education, Fresno, CA, 1996.
37. Lazear, David, *Seven Ways of Knowing: Teaching for Multiple Intelligences*, Palatine, IL: IRI/Skylight Publishing, 1991.
38. Schifini, Alfredo. "Sheltered Instruction: The Basics," *Getting the Picture*, Los Angeles County Office of Education/RETAC, 1994, p. 2:5.
39. Schifini, Alfredo. "Cornerstones of Sheltered Instruction," *Getting the Picture*, Los Angeles County Office of Education, 1994, p. 2:7-8
40. "A Guide for Curricular Planning" in Appendix B is an additional resource for the instructional planning team to create effective lessons for all students.

Chapter 7

Information Literacy in Action:
Sample Scenarios

▼ Chapter 7 • Sample Scenarios

Search Scenarios

The essence of the search process is the ability to recognize a problem, analyze it, and then act to resolve it. The scenarios that follow describe situations, both curricular and personal, in which students are involved in a search process. They are intended to illustrate a sampling of the infinite variety of ways in which groups and individuals might think and respond in problem-solving situations.

The scenarios follow students and teachers as they:

- Identify – or stumble onto – a problem or question that requires a search for information.
- Work collaboratively to accomplish their task.
- Use a wide variety of resources that include people, places, print, and technology.
- Extend their searches beyond school to homes, communities, and other worlds.
- Reflect and assess what they have learned from the search process.
- Use the combination of languages most appropriate for their needs in accessing, evaluating, and presenting or applying information.

1. Owl in Distress

Scenario

The tank trucks leave a thick layer of black tarry road oil on a dirt road. The two families in the cabins on either side of the road have been warned to leave their cars beyond where the oiling would take place and not to walk on it for 24 hours. The next morning Allie and Robert, nine and seven-year-old weekend visitors, go out to look at the road and find a bird mired, covered with tar, and exhausted.

Explore/identify the need for information. This bird looks half dead. Can we save it? Who can tell us what we need to do? What kind of bird is it?

Identify potential resources. Their father, an avid city-dweller, has no idea of what to do, but recognizes the need to do something quickly. Don, the man across the street, lives here all the time and might have some better idea of how to care for ailing wildlife. They could also look in the phone book for the number of a veterinarian, or some public service agency for animals.

Develop general search strategies to refine the question. Going back to the cabin and looking in the phone book would take time. They decide to go and get Don and take him to the bird while Allie runs to get some newspaper to wrap the bird.

Information Literacy

Locate and explore resources; select specific resources and formulate search strategies for using them. The children's father, has an idea to use paint thinner, but before they try it, Don suggests they call a veterinarian and see what he says. Better to take the time than make a fatal mistake.

Locate, analyze, and select information needed. They look in the phone book for some government agency that might help, like a department of animal control, but find nothing under state or county. They try the Humane Society, but there is no answer because it is a weekend. Finally, they try one of the veterinarians listed.

Evaluate information retrieved; determine relevance. Don thinks that since it is petroleum they ought to try detergent, and the vet agrees. Paint thinner would be toxic and damage the bird's skin. He tells them the bird will be very dehydrated and to try to give it water with an eyedropper. He also tells them to keep it warm.

Determine how to use information. They put some warm water in a tub with detergent and begin sponging the bird repeatedly. Its big yellow eyes are all that they have been able to see as proof of life, as they open and close. They can feel its heart beat. After uncounted washings, most of the oil is gone, but the bird is very weak and just lies in the box they have prepared. They begin to give the bird water with the eyedropper and it tries to drink.

Evaluate results; evaluate process. The bird survives and after a while stands on Don's gloved hand. It has talons, beak, and big round eyes. It makes a clicking noise with its beak and moves its head from side to side as it looks at its benefactors. It must be an owl. What kind is it?

Identify potential resources. They look in the indexes of their bird books under owls. There are many different kinds, but the only one that seems to match their bird in size is the pygmy owl. Later that day, when they go into town for groceries, they find a book in the library about a pygmy owl, called *Owl* by William Service (Knopf, 1969).

Locate, analyze, select information, evaluate information retrieved, determine relevance, determine how to use. Don checks the book out on his library card; the book is not only interesting and funny, but also contains a great deal of information about how to care for and feed the feisty, determined bird they have found and befriended.

▼ Chapter 7 • Sample Scenarios

2. How Much Should We Charge?

Scenario

As a fund-raising project to get additional computer software, the class decided to sell cans of nuts that a parent offered to provide at a discount.

Explore/identify the need for information. To give the students background in fund-raising, the teacher showed "To Buy or Not to Buy," from the ITV series *Trade Offs*. This program presented students with such concepts as what happens when your price is too high for the market and how competition can limit your sales.

Formulate the questions. As a follow-up to the video, students were organized into teams to determine what price would sell the most cans and give the greatest profit.

Identify potential resources. Students identified tasks to provide them with information. These were: (1) contacting another class with experience in fund-raising, (2) surveying newspaper ads and store price surveys, (3) checking the library for books and magazines that might have techniques for organizing selling, and developing a market survey (as suggested in the videotaping).

Locate and explore resources; develop general search strategies to refine the questions. Teams developed strategies for each task group. They identified key words to expedite their library and online search of books, periodicals, and company web sites, e.g., sales, marketing, competition, pricing, fund raising, marketing surveys. They developed a list of questions to use in contacting other fund-raising groups, designed a check sheet to compare current prices, and designed a survey sheet to determine the market for their product. They used the computer software program called "Hot Dog Stand"(in Survival Math by Sunburst) which introduced additional variables to consider when setting a price.

Evaluate information retrieved; determine relevance. After using these instruments to obtain the necessary information, a decision was made on the price that would give them the highest profit per can. Students test-marketed for one week and discovered sales were slower than they had anticipated. After reviewing the situation, they lowered the price per can and sales increased.

3. Relating Literature to Life

Scenario

After reading *So Far From the Bamboo Grove* by Kawashima Watkins (Lothrop), an autobiographical novel about the flight of two Japanese daughters and their mother from Korea to Kyoto, Japan at the end of World War II, Mrs. Thompson decided that reading books like this would be one way to make World War II come alive for the students in her 9th grade world history class.

Explore/identify the need for information; Identify potential resources. Mrs. Thompson planned to use the "into, through, beyond" approach to the teaching of literature. With the help of other teachers and the librarians in the school and public libraries, a good sized list of books having to do with ordinary, non-military people during World War II was compiled.

To set the tone, she would read aloud two serious and moving picture books about children in Japan and Europe during the war. *Hiroshima No Pika* by Toshi Maruke (Lothrop) and *Rose Blanche* by Innocenti (Stewart Tabori & Chang). After a general class discussion about war and its consequences for ordinary people and innocent bystanders, she would distribute a list of related books and comment on each of them. Each student would choose a book to read.

Locate, analyze, and select information needed. She would ask them to keep dialectical journals (comments on specific, self-chosen, portions of the text) while reading their books, keeping in mind the written and oral project they would do when finished.

Evaluate information retrieved; determine relevance. Hoping for questions and ideas provoked by their reading and dialectical journals, she would ask for a short research report that would attempt to answer their most pressing questions. She knew that for many of them that would be difficult, but with the help of the school and public librarians who had also read many of the books, she hoped to be able to help them focus on important ideas. Interviews with people who lived during the time of the story, who served in the armed forces in World War II, or those in the community familiar with the customs and philosophy of the people and country involved would be valuable. Online visits to web sites highlighting World War II and its aftermath would add to the students' resource base.

Identify valuable resources. To obtain information on their selected topic, students brainstormed lists of potential resources similar to the following:

- People who lived in Japan, Germany, etc. during the time of the story
- People who served in the armed forces during World War II

- People in the community familiar with the customs and philosophy of various ethnic groups
- School and public libraries and museums
- Embassies
- Online databases, mailing lists, and usenet newsgroups

Develop general search strategies to refine questions. Four forms of exploration were chosen:
- Students prepared questions for interviews of selected community members and learned interview techniques.
- Students wrote letters of inquiry to embassies.
- Teacher and students met with the librarian to plan further research.
- Students researched web sites and looked for further people contacts.

Select specific resources and formulate search strategies for using them; locate, analyze, and select information needed; evaluate information retrieved; determine relevance. Working in pairs in the library media center, students selected appropriate materials from library resources and recorded pertinent information. Those students on interview teams arranged and recorded information from interviews. Useful responses from embassies were selected.

Determine how to use/present/communicate information. The drama of what they read, combined with the interviews they held with community members, inspired many with the desire to simulate oral interviews with the characters in their novels and biographies. They felt this would be an effective way of sharing with other students their own intense experiences.

Evaluate results; evaluate process. So, what is worthwhile about reading books like *So Far From the Bamboo Grove?* The vividness of the experiences, the reality of the characters, the recreation of a period of history in a vital personal way. The project seemed to be a general success. The difficult part was the one Mrs. Thompson anticipated: getting at the ideas, themes, and questions of each novel. Some succeeded better than others, of course, but all who participated came away with a more intense awareness of the lives of people during World War II, and that was the purpose of the project.

4. Where Do I Begin?

Scenario

Mr. Marker is a creative social studies teacher who gives students choices about assignments. He alerted me that he was sending Robbie, an eighth grader, for help with a pending oral exam on the Vietnam War, a topic that seemed to be swallowing him with its complexities.

Explore/identify the need for information.

"Mr. Marker sent me up here to get a book about the Vietnam War," Robbie said.

"Do you just need a little information, or are you going to write a report, or what?" I asked.

"Well, it's 10% of my grade and I have to know everything ... how we got in, how we got out, and what happened after."

"Are you going to write something?"

"No, he's going to ask me a bunch of questions. When he asked this other guy questions and he answered right, Mr. Marker said he'd showed he'd read a book. So I need a book."

"What do you know about it already? Do you know when it began or ended?"

"I know when it ended ... 1973 ... I think. I figure if I read a book about it, I'll find out everything."

"Do you have time to talk about it? Maybe I can help you get started. 'Let's sit down and see if we can make a plan, figure out a strategy so you can do a really good job and get full credit. Where do you think a good place to begin would be?'"

"The computer catalog? To find a book about it? I think a book would be proof that I'd done some work on it ... to back up my answers."

"How about getting some basic information about the whole war? Do you think that's a good idea?"

"No, I think I just need a book."

"Well the bad news is that the ninth graders have been here ahead of you, and I don't think there's one book left here or at the public library. Do you have a lot of time before you have your oral exam?"

He did have plenty of time so I set out to convince him that he needed a plan of action, that possibly reading a book wouldn't be enough. If the book were too old, it wouldn't tell him as much as he needed to know. It might be one sided. He might need to read more books than he had time for.

Formulate questions. Between us, we brainstormed what he knew and I added a few ideas. While we talked, I showed him how to cluster these ideas. As we

▼ Chapter 7 • Sample Scenarios

did it, he began to indicate that there was a lot he would need to know, more than he thought.

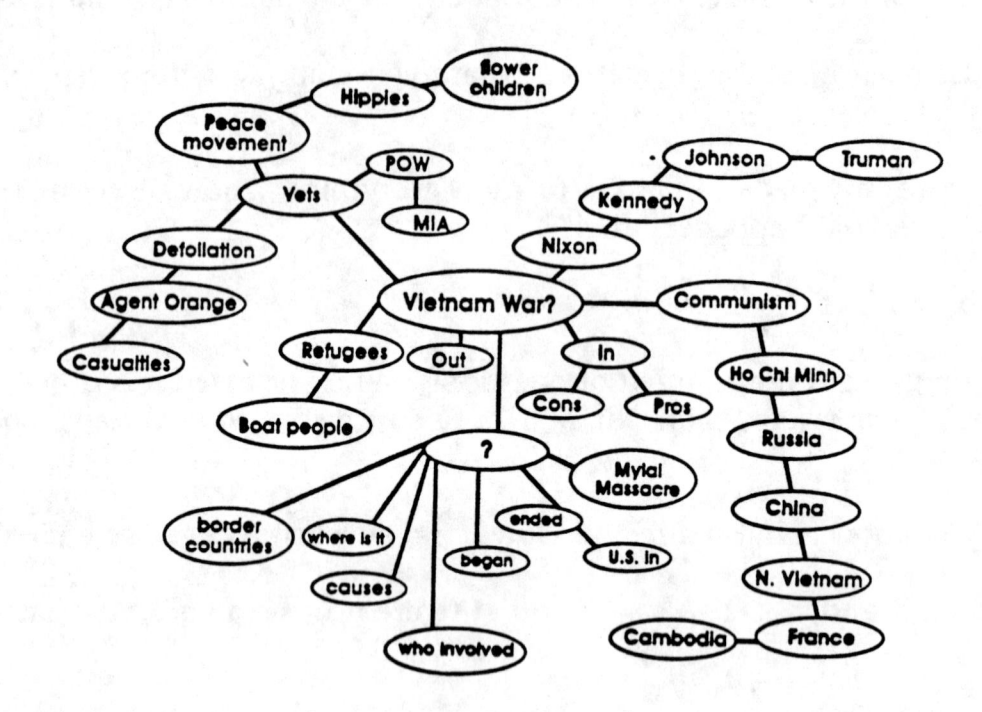

```
                    flower
            Hippies  children
      Peace
    movement            Johnson — Truman
            POW    Kennedy
       Vets
            MIA   Nixon
   Defoliation            Communism
  Agent Orange  Vietnam War?
                                Ho Chi Minh
   Casualties  Refugees  Out  In
                    Cons  Pros   Russia
     Boat people    ?
                         Myla
                       Massacre  China
   border       ended
   countries where is it        N. Vietnam
          began      U.S. in
          causes
                            Cambodia — France
        who involved
```

Identify potential resources. We talked about some resources he might use to find out something such as a print or electronic encyclopedia, an atlas, maybe some biographical dictionaries, books, periodicals and online databases. He thought he might be able to talk to some people who might have information. Maybe he would see some movies, like *Platoon* and *Hanoi Hilton* too.

Develop general search strategies to refine the questions.

"And what will you look under in the reference books?"

"Vietnam War." He looked at me as if to say, what else?

"Let's look and see."

When we did, we came up with some synonyms and allied subjects, e.g., Vietnam, Vietnamese Conflict. In *World Almanac* alone, we found 26 possible topics to research. *World Book Encyclopedia*, with back-to-back articles on the country and the war, provided dozens more. While he could see that *World Book* told more than he needed, it provided a good background. He felt he would need to memorize a good bit of material to answer Mr. Marker's questions.

"What kind of questions will he ask you?" I asked. Robbie really didn't know if he had to have names, dates, statistics, battles, places memorized. He realized it would be important to know that before he went too far.

Locate and explore resources. Looking at it laid out in the almanac and encyclopedia made it seem less formidable. Now when he did read his books (when the ninth graders finally returned them) he would have a better idea of what was important to know. Finding out Mr. Marker's expectations would help too.

Robbie learned about a variety of resources including *Newsbank, Facts on File,* and some biographical dictionaries he had not used before. He was really pleased to learn that when he searched some sources on CD-ROM, he was able to print out the full text of articles or other material he was looking for. He also became reacquainted with some old standbys he knew at least by sight ... almanacs, encyclopedias, atlases, the vertical file, and the dictionary. He listed the other places and people who could help him: the public library, relatives, and perhaps the veterans organizations.

Select specific resources and formulate search strategies for using them. After he talked to Mr. Marker, he found out that there were some facts he would have to memorize, but not as many as he thought. He now knew what to concentrate on, what questions were important, and how to go about finding the answers.

- How and when did the U.S. get involved in the Vietnam War?
- When did they get out? When did the war end?
- What was the outcome? the aftermath?
  - for South Vietnam, North Vietnam?
  - for the refugees?
  - for the veterans, prisoners, MIAs?
  - for the United States?
  - for China, Thailand, Kampuchea (Cambodia), etc.?

The resources he chose to use included:

- *The World Almanac*
- *World Book Encyclopedia*
- Atlas
- *Magazine Article Summaries*
- *Facts on File*
- Various trade books
- Interview with relative who is a veteran

Evaluate results; evaluate process. Robbie discovered that beginning with the *World Almanac,* which became his framework, everything he read filled in and fleshed out what he knew. By the time he finished reading, gathering, and discarding data, he had a good grasp on the background and outcome of the Vietnam War. His oral presentation and exam by Mr. Marker, in front of the rest of his class, were well received by teacher and students. He more than earned the final 10% of his grade.

5. Waste Disposal Plant

Scenario

Students in an industrial technology class at Anytown High School in Anytown, U.S.A., were quite concerned about the arguments in the newspaper regarding the waste disposal plant to be located one mile from their community. Arguments in favor of the location of the plant included: 1) the land was already owned by the city; 2) the local dump was near capacity, 3) the closest residential area was at least a mile away; and 4) the plant, which would incinerate solid waste, was expected to create 250 much needed jobs in the community. The arguments against the location were: 1) although the plant was a mile from their community, prevailing winds would blow the pollution directly at it; and 2) the design for the plant did not include technology for the maximum efficiency, and there would be more air pollution than necessary. A hearing before the city council was scheduled for the next month with several strategy planning meetings in the community before. The students thought if they could submit a design that might improve the efficiency of the plant, maybe everyone would win.

Explore/identify the need for information. The students needed to access the plans for the proposed waste disposal plant. They needed a copy of the environmental impact study. They wanted to review all the public discussion that had occurred to date. They needed to understand how other communities had dealt with the problem of solid waste disposal.

Formulate questions. What have people in our community and other communities said and/or written about solid waste disposal? What are the pros and cons of the type of plant currently under consideration? How have other communities dealt with the air pollution question?

Relate the question to prior knowledge. The teacher encouraged the students to keep logs on their discussions while working on the project in order to document where they went for information, their thoughts about the project, and any other relevant items. The students first brainstormed everything they knew about waste disposal. They listed all the reasons they could think of for and against the incinerator method. They suggested other ways of disposing of the trash from their community and discussed the feasibility of these methods.

Identify potential resources. Potential resources for background on solid waste disposal were reference books, magazines, newspapers, and indexes (hard copy and electronic) for these materials. The city planning office might be able to provide them with copies of the environmental impact study and plans for the waste disposal plant.

Develop general search strategies to refine the questions. The students asked the library media specialist for assistance when they could not find everything they needed in the library catalog and periodical indexes. He helped them use *Sears' List of Subject Headings* and the *Library of Congress List of Subject Headings* to isolate appropriate subject headings to search under. He also helped them select a full-text newspaper database and *Pollution Abstracts* from Dialog Information Services for local and general information on waste management. The library media center also had a subscription to *Biology Digest,* an index with abstracts of articles in popular and scientific magazines on all types of scientific subjects. A call to the city planning office helped them find out how to obtain the reports they wanted.

Locate, analyze, and select information needed. Several newspapers across the country had articles on problems that were similar to those of Anytown. The students were able to understand the arguments for and against the type of waste disposal plant suggested for their area. Starting with popular magazines' treatments of the problem and working up to the scientific magazines' discussions helped the students see that there were other alternatives to the type of plant that had been proposed. Information about the wind patterns in their area also enabled them to suggest a different orientation of the exhaust mechanism that would minimize the amount of air pollution coming into the community.

Analyze information retrieved; determine its relevance. The students found information about how communities similar to theirs handled the problem. They found different ways to construct waste disposal plants.

Determine how to communicate information. The students wrote a careful report citing facts and figures describing all the pros and cons they were able to find about solid waste disposal plants, air and other types of pollution emanating from the operation, and how to minimize the negative effects of such an operation. They presented their figures using slides produced by a computer program. Using their computer-aided drafting (CAD) skills, they drew plans for another plant, making changes they thought would help both sides of the conflict come to a resolution. They applied for and were granted time to make their presentation orally at the community hearing before the City Council.

Evaluate results; evaluate process. The students' presentation was well-received. In reviewing their logs, they were surprised to see how much they had learned.

▼ Chapter 7 • Sample Scenarios

6. Brainstorming Resources

Scenario

Sandy Schuckett, a library media specialist in Los Angeles Unified School District with a majority of English learners, wanted to explore what sources of information her students were aware of or were already using. She and the classroom teacher generated a list of questions that they thought would engage students' thinking.

Identify potential resources. Sandy organized the students into collaborative groups to brainstorm the answers to the questions. Here are Sandy's comments:

> Before we dealt with the "engaging questions," I asked them generally where they would go to find information. Their answers were books, dictionary, library, encyclopedia, newspaper, TV, phone, radio, friends, teachers, police, family, scientists, doctors.... I thought that was a good range of sources before we even got into any kind of discussion about finding information. Once they got their questions, it was interesting to note that even though this was a relatively advanced ESL class, they did all of the discussion with their partners in Spanish! However, they wrote out their lists in English. I decided to repeat the same activity again with an intermediate level ESL class, totally in Spanish — sort of a "control group." I followed exactly the same procedure as with the previous class.

Following are some of the situations Sandy posed and student responses about where they would go to find information.

- You have written some stories, and your ESL teacher tells you that they are very good and that you should try to get them published.

Bookstore, library, teacher, publisher's office. (I thought this was pretty astute! I've had adults ask me this same question without even a clue of the answer!)

- You are going to baby-sit for your neighbor. It is the first time you will actually be paid for doing this, and you want to do the best possible job.

Preguntarle a mi mamá. Preguntarlés a los vecinos. Preguntarles a los adultos. Ver la T.V. Leer revistas. En libros. En guarderías. (Ask my mom. Ask the neighbors. Ask other adults. Watch TV. Read magazines. In books. At the nursery schools.)

- Someone in your best friend's family has a terrible disease, and she is worried that it might be hereditary and that she might get it too.

Information Literacy

Hospital, doctor, enfermero/enfermera, clínica, gente grande, farmacéutico, curandera. (The hospital, doctor, nurses, doctor's offices, grownups, pharmacy, folkhealer.)

- You and your friends want to start a drama club and put on a play.

Periódicos, la guía telefónica, revistas, televisión, libros, radio, adultos, amigos, familiares, maestro, barrios, actores, estudiante de teatro. (newspapers, phone book, magazines, television, books, radio, adults, friends, relatives, teachers, neighborhood, actors, drama students.)

Select the most useful resources for further exploration; evaluate results. Sandy confirmed for herself and her students that they were already familiar with many valid sources of information. She and their teacher would collaborate on appropriate next steps for helping them to explore these resources and to identify useful resources beyond these familiar ones.

7. Picturing History

Joyce Roth, in her work with the California History-Social Science Project, demonstrates to teachers how photographs can be used as primary sources to reveal extensive information. She suggests the following as a scenario for helping students to think more deeply about the lives of people during the Gold Rush:

In the 1840's, gold was discovered in the hills of what later became California. Many men left their families and migrated westward seeking fortunes. Why did a majority of men come alone? For clues, look at photos of miners on location. Questions that you might want to ask are . . .

Where is this place? How would you describe the landscape? Is this place flat or mountainous, dry or wet? What natural features do you see? How has the environment been touched by humans? Are there buildings? If so, what kinds and for what purposes? How does one travel to, from, and in this region?

Now that you have analyzed the photo once or twice, why do you think most men came alone or with other men to the gold fields? Put yourself in this photo. How would you be living? Describe your feelings. Suppose you were the miner there alone.

Now think of other questions that you have. Write them in your journal. Refer back to them and continually add to them.

Compare pictures of this region with those of life in the East during the same time period. Use a Venn diagram to record notes about characteristics of life at that time that are similar and dissimilar.

We can see that the land plays a significant role in determining the historical story. Based upon your research using photos, how do you think life changed for many children during the gold rush?

What other resources should you gather and use to expand your view? Remember that one photo provides only one picture of the way things were. Many photos will allow you to make some assumptions; adding excerpts from diaries, tapes of oral interviews, and investigating artifacts will further clarify the authenticity of your ideas.

Based upon your conclusions, support or refute this statement: "Miners were greedy people."

8. Identifying an Audience and a Reason to Write[2]

English-as-second-language (ESL) students have a wealth of experiences to share with native English speakers. One of the most interesting and most immediate experiences they can draw on and translate into a narrative is the story of their departure or their parents' departure from their homeland and their journey to the United States.

At the prewriting stage we have a discussion about these students' experiences. Many of them have traveled extensively, seen other parts of the world, lived in cultures with different customs, and so forth. I point out to the ESL students that many Americans would love to meet and talk with them and find out where they came from because most Americans have little information about their country's most recent immigrants.

As a prewriting exercise, I tell the students that a whole book has been written about immigrants traveling to the United States; their experiences are also worth sharing. I then read a selection from *American Dreams: Lost and Found*, by Studs Terkel. It is an account of Dora Rosenzweig, a Russian immigrant. Dora's story becomes the model for my students' own narrative.

After I read this excerpt from *American Dreams*, we discuss what Dora said and identify what we think would be interesting to United States citizens. Before we begin to write, I ask for the students' input about what should be discussed in the narrative in sequential order, and I write their suggestions on the chalkboard. For instance, we begin asking questions that we believe people would most like to have answered:

1. How long ago did this event take place?
2. How did you learn that you would be moving?
3. What was your life like before you left?
4. How did you actually escape or move?

5. With whom did you travel?
6. What was your travel experience like?
7. Were there any problems or exciting experiences?

Next, I tell the students to write only what they feel comfortable with sharing and to give as accurate an account as they can so that their audience can picture their experiences. I also tell them that only I will know the authors' true identities. To provide some structure for their reminiscences, I ask the students to write about their family life first, followed by their traveling and immigration experiences, and finally how they feel about life in the United States.

Because my students already have a wealth of memories to tap in telling their stories, they can focus less on what they want to say and put their energy into how they will say it. Providing an interested audience for them – a classmate at school, new neighbor, supportive teacher – and a topic they have deep feelings about motivates them to communicate as clearly and descriptively as they are able. Once they relate their experiences on paper in this new language, they can read them aloud in small groups or work individually with the teacher to make any necessary corrections.

9. Sharing Languages and Organizing Data[3]

Scenario

In Mr. Martinez's fifth-grade class, most of the students are native Spanish speakers who are learning English as the other students in the class are learning Spanish. The class meets once a week for conversation with a high school Spanish class, an opportunity for mutual help and enjoyment in acquiring each other's languages.

As part of their science curriculum, the fifth-grade students have been engaged in some interesting activities designed to help them to expand their understanding of the concept of data analysis and appreciate its value in the scientific process. Since many of the students have pets, they decide to create a simple database with as much information as they can gather about their pets. In this way they will be able to sort and display their data. They also decide to invite their high school partners to participate in this project. The high school students can contribute data about their own pets, thereby providing more data to use and compare.

First, students work in small groups to decide what fields should be included in the pet database. Obvious fields are student's name, pet's name, animal species, age of pet, height and weight of pet, color, food the pet eats, housing (cage, box, kennel, and so forth), and distinguishing characteristics, such as number of legs or the sounds the pet makes. The field names are in both English and Spanish, with data being entered in either language, or both.

During a meeting with their high school partners, students begin to ask additional questions about their pets. What breed of animal is it? In what country did this breed of animal originate? Has this pet ever played a role as a helper to humans? This activity sets the pattern for gathering and using data. Students comb their communities for information and interview their families and friends. It becomes a challenge to see who can find a new and fascinating fact about a chosen pet.

The library media specialist works with the classroom teacher to guide students through their research process. Students identify key words and create a web for each category of pets. In a jigsaw, students begin to explore specific library resources for information on pets and then report what they found in English and Spanish encyclopedias, nonfiction books, magazines, CD-ROM and online sources. Many bring information from both English- and Spanish-language newspapers and magazines from home.

As new information is located, it becomes necessary to revise some database field names and to add several new fields. Students begin to experiment with sorting the data on various fields in the database. They also discover the many different report formats they can print.

As a follow-up to this project, students used the computer word-processing program, The Bilingual Writing Center, to prepare a Spanish-English bilingual book based on the information they gathered. Copies of the book were added to the library collections at each school.

10. Radio DJs: A Constructivist Internet Lesson

Carol Lang, a consultant in Telecommunications and Technology with the Los Angeles County Office of Education, designed the following project to demonstrate to teachers how they might guide students in an open-ended but purposeful use of the Internet for personal decision making.

When using the Internet or any form of technology, gathering new and interesting information and/or resources can lead a student into thinking that "The Answer" has been found. The goal of this lesson is to guide students into learning new ways of thinking, not just learning new facts — concepts, not keystrokes. Learners need to ask themselves, "So what is the value of the information?" "Why is it important?" Teachers need to focus on type of thinking they want the students to accomplish.

This lesson was designed to be fun for students and present a reason for an authentic investigation. It is framed so that specific kinds of thinking (organization, analysis, synthesis, etc.) are required of the students. The format is adapted from Apple Computer's Unit of Practice model.

The problem:

Your parents are radio DJs in Los Angeles and they have been offered jobs in Buffalo, Ft. Lauderdale, and St. Paul. Since they know that you understand how to use the Internet, they have asked you to work together, conduct research and make recommendation for where your family should relocate.

Family members: Kevin and Mrs. Bean and their children, Alanis, Doug (The Slug), and Cranberry. Alanis has a boyfriend in Los Angeles, and therefore, doesn't want to move but hates earthquakes. Doug wants to be near the beach and doesn't like to be where it is cold. Cranberry likes to snowboard. The radio station where your parents have been working has been sold and is becoming an all-classical station. They need a new gig in a new city. Where should they go?

Goal (teacher's curriculum-design challenge)

To move students from just gathering to assessing and judging information. A lot of raw data is available through the Internet, but it needs to be applied in a meaningful way to solve a problem.

Tasks (nature of student actions)

1. Predict what you think your recommendation might be and why. (Use prior learning.)
2. Decide on a plan of action. (global)
3. What information is available? How much is enough? What's important?
4. Break the plan into action items. Move from a topic to questions to be answered. (narrow) What are some factors to research? (cost of living, weather, earthquakes, etc.) What's the best way to get the information? (e-mail to the Chamber of Commerce for tourism information, e-mail to a school and ask for impressions, web browser to collect temperature and rainfall data, gopher to get news articles, etc.) How are you going to organize the information? How are you going to cite references? (database, brochure for each city, advertisement for each city, etc.)
5. Value the items. Do all the factors carry the same weight? What are the priorities? How do you know? (sort in a database, prioritize in a spreadsheet, etc.) How are you going to weigh the factors? (spreadsheet, type size, etc.)
6. Visualize and analyze the information. What trends or problems do you see? (chart, graphs, etc.) Address concerns of the family members. What are the differences and similarities in the children's and adults' concerns? (word process their feelings)

7. Consider constraints. Are there any factors that would prevent or discourage them from going to a city? (list, budget, etc.)
8. Be open to other factors. What are their implications?
9. Make a recommendation. Please show the process, factors and rationale used in arriving at your recommendation.

Assessment (criteria for evaluating students' work)
- Each member works to the best of his or her ability.
- Steps are completed.
- Complete information is provided.
- A system is devised for assigning values.
- Information is translated into clear, concrete representations.
- Sensitivity is communicated in considering feelings.
- Recommendations are supported by the factors.
- The project is evaluated using self assessment, team assessment, and peer (class) review.

NOTES

1. Adapted with permission from a scenario originally developed by Oregon New Standards Project Team for Applied Learning, 1992.
2. This scenario is taken from: *Practical Ideas for Teaching Writing as a Process at the High School and College Levels*, California Department of Education, 1997, p. 109.
3. Acknowledgment: The California Telemation Project.
4. Article by Amy Pule, *Times* education writer, "History in the Making," *Los Angeles Times*, June 4, 1995.

RUBRICS

for the

Assessment

of

Information Literacy[1]

A companion to the
Information Literacy Rubrics
for
School Library Media Specialists

State Library and Adult Education Office
201 E. Colfax Avenue
Denver, CO 80203

CEMA
Colorado Educational Media Association

1996

---

[1] Reprinted with permission.

An Overview and Framework for the Information Literacy Rubrics

Target Indicators	In Progress	Essential	Proficient	Advanced
Student as a Knowledge Seeker	• I need someone to tell me when I need information, what information I need, and help me find it.	• Sometimes I can identify my information needs. I ask for help finding and using information.	• I am able to determine when I have a need for information. I often solve problems by using a variety of information resources.	• I know my information needs. I am confident that I can solve problems by selecting and processing information.
Student as a Quality Producer	• Someone else sets the standards and I try to create a product to meet them.	• I may need help understanding what makes a good product, and support to create it.	• I compare my work to models and use them as an example for my product.	• I hold high standards for my work and create quality products.
Student as a Self-Directed Learner	• I have trouble choosing my own resources and I like someone to tell me the answer.	• I might know what I want, but need to ask for help in solving information problems.	• I choose my own resources and like being independent in my information searches.	• I like to choose my own information resources. I am comfortable in situations where there are multiple answers as well as those with no answers.
Student as a Group Contributor	• I need support to work in a group. I have trouble taking responsibility to help the group.	• I usually participate with the group. I offer opinions and ideas, but can not always defend them. I rely on others to make group decisions.	• I participate effectively as a group member. I help the group process, and evaluate and use information with the group.	• I am comfortable leading, facilitating, negotiating, or participating in a group. I work with others to create a product that fairly represents consensus of the group.
Student as a Responsible Information User	• If I find information I can use I copy it directly. I need to be reminded about being polite and about sharing resources and equipment with others.	• I usually remember to give credit when I use someone else's ideas. It is okay for others to have different ideas from mine. I try to be polite and share information resources and equipment with others.	• I do not plagiarize. I understand the concept of intellectual freedom. I am polite and share resources and equipment with others.	• I follow copyright laws and guidelines. I help others understand the concept of intellectual freedom, and can defend my rights if challenged. I acknowledge and respect the rights of others to use information resources and equipment.

Students as Knowledge Seekers: Information Guideline #1 (Part 2)

Target Indicators	In Progress	Essential	Proficient	Advanced
Organizes Information	• I try to organize information, but have trouble and have to ask for help. • I need to be reminded to credit sources.	• I know some ways to organize information. I can use one or two very well. • Sometimes I credit sources appropriately.	• I organize information in different ways. • I usually credit sources appropriately.	• I choose to organize information in a way that matches my learning style and/or to best meet my information needs. • I always credit sources appropriately.
Processes Information	• I put information together without processing it.	• I combine information to create meaning. I draw conclusions.	• I integrate information from a variety of sources to create meaning that connects with prior knowledge. I can draw conclusions on my own from my sources.	• I integrate information to create meaning that connects with prior knowledge and draw clear and appropriate conclusions. I provide specific and supportive details.
Acts on Information	• I am not sure what actions to take based on my information needs. • I ask for help to find everything I need.	• I know what to do with the information I find. • Some of the information I find is appropriate to my needs.	• I act based on the information I have collected and processed. • I do this in a way that is appropriate to my needs.	• I act independently of the information I have collected and processed. • I do this in a way that is appropriate to my needs. I can explain my actions so that others understand.
Evaluates Process and Product	• I don't know how I did. I need someone to help me figure out how to improve.	• I know how well I did and have a few ideas on how to improve next time.	• I know when I've done a good job, and know when there are things I could have done better. I make some revisions.	• I evaluate the product and the process throughout my work, and make revisions when necessary.

Students as Self-Directed Learners: Information Guideline #3

Target Indicators	In Progress	Essential	Proficient	Advanced
Voluntarily Establishes Clear Information Goals and Manages Progress	• Setting information goals is difficult for me. • I need help from someone to choose what I'm supposed to do. • I work best with problems that have only one answer.	• I can set some information goals by myself. • I can sometimes find what I'm supposed to do on my own. • I see that sometimes there may be more than one solution for my project or problem.	• I almost always set my own information goals. • I can usually find a variety of information resources to achieve those goals. • When there is more than one solution, I choose the appropriate one for my project or problem.	• I can set my own information goals, and choose the best way to achieve them. • I like to explore and evaluate various resources and solutions. I use them to create a new solution to the problem. • I'm comfortable in situations where there are multiple answers, or no "best" answer.
Voluntarily Consults Media Sources	• I usually use the easiest source, and only one source.	• I can do what is asked of me, and usually find answers to questions after consulting a few sources.	• I understand how different sources are organized, and look for the ones that best meet my needs.	• I look at many different sources to find those that meet my needs. I consider various point-of-view and the merits of the resources before choosing those that work best for me.
Explores Topics of Interest	• I have trouble enjoying my reading, and have a hard time staying with a book -- or other reading material. • I tend to over-use certain information resources to the exclusion of others when I do read. • I have trouble exploring new topics. Someone needs to help me get started.	• I enjoy reading certain types of books and other information resources. • I usually read only about one subject, or stay with one author's works. • I explore new topics when required.	• I like reading several different types of literature. • I enjoy reading in a variety of formats (e.g. books, CD-ROM, and other media). • I read to explore and learn about a variety of topics.	• Reading is very important to me, and I enjoy reading and exploring many different topics. • I use information resources for information and personal needs, and actively seek answers to questions. • I consider alternative perspectives and evaluate differing points-of-view. • I read for pleasure, to learn, and to solve problems
Identifies and Applies Personal Performance	• I just do what I'm told. Someone tells me if it's good or not.	• I know when I've done a good job.	• I know when I've done a good job, and know why I was successful. I am satisfied with the results.	• I know how I learn best, and can choose the method(s) which guarantees my success. I can evaluate what I've done. I'm not always satisfied with my results.

Students as Responsible Information Users: Information Guideline 5

Target Indicators	In Progress	Essential	Proficient	Advanced
Practices Ethical Usage of Information and Information Sources	• I don't give credit to others when I use their information. • I don't know why some things need quote marks, and have trouble putting information in my own words. • I don't know why I can't use other people's work (from books, or other information resources).	• I can usually put information in my own words. • If I use someone else's words, I usually remember to put them in quotes. • I can create a bibliography to credit my sources, and don't copy other people's work. • I know it's against the law to copy computer disks, tapes, or other materials.	• I follow copyright laws and guidelines by giving credit to all quotes and ideas, citing them in notes and bibliography properly. • I only make copies of print, software, or tapes when I can locate permission from the author/publisher, or by locating permission on the materials.	• I understand and appreciate that copyright protects the creator of the resource, so I always follow and uphold copyright regulations. • I do not plagiarize. • I cite all my sources by following a format demonstrated to me by a teacher or other source. • When I need to copy something, I know how to, and do get permission from the copyright holder.
Respects Principle of Intellectual Freedom	• I usually don't pay attention to what others read, listen to, or view, and sometimes react inappropriately to them.	• I don't try to keep someone from expressing their own ideas, nor reading, listening to, or viewing what they want.	• I understand it is important to have many and differing perspectives on a subject. • I know I have the right to express my opinion, and usually offer my opinion in an appropriate manner.	• I can explain my First Amendment rights, and if challenged, know the process available to me to defend those rights. • I promote the rights of others, and defend them as well.

Appendix B

Research Process Competencies Planning Guide

Appendix B: Research Process Competencies: A Planning Guide

Planning Space

Competencies

B. Focus the purpose of the research by formulating a specific question to be answered.
C. Develop a preliminary central question or thesis statement.

3: RELATE QUESTION TO PRIOR KNOWLEDGE; IDENTIFY KEY WORDS, CONCEPTS, AND NAMES

A. Record previous knowledge relating to the central question.
  1. Quickwrite.
  2. Brainstorm ideas and information about the central question by recalling previous experiences.
  3. Note key words, concepts, and names related to the search question.
  4. Demonstrate the ability to use strategies such as the following to organize known information: list, cluster, traditional outline, mind map, radial outline, other organizing strategies.
B. Review research process journal to determine missing elements.
C. When previous knowledge is limited, use general sources of information to focus on relationships and key terms for overview of topic:
  1. Skim chapters in books, encyclopedia articles,

Information Literacy   145

Appendix B: Research Process Competencies: A Planning Guide

Competencies	Planning Space
5: DEVELOP GENERAL SEARCH STRATEGIES TO ORGANIZE THE SEARCH A. Use previously compiled terms and add subject headings and database descriptors which relate to the central question or thesis. B. Summarize in simple sentence form the main ideas regarding the central question. C. Ask further questions to clarify meaning. D. Construct sub-questions about the central question. E. Discriminate between more important and less important questions and exclude the least important questions. F. Create a plan for the search based on the resulting questions. G. Organize key words, phrases, and subject headings into Boolean and other relevant search strategies (See pp. 47-53, for further explanation). H. Reanalyze search strategies as success or failure is experienced.	

Information Literacy

Appendix B: Research Process Competencies: A Planning Guide

Competencies	Planning Space
4. Use subject headings and cross references to find additional resources.	
5. Access relevant records in electronic databases.	
a. Determine the possible databases to be searched.	
b. Design the search strategy, narrowing or expanding the search parameters as needed.	
C. Revise or redefine the central question as necessary.	
7: SELECT THE MOST USEFUL RESOURCES FOR FURTHER EXPLORATION AND FORMULATE SPECIFIC STRATEGIES FOR USING THEM	
A. Select the most useful resources from those available.	
1. Skim the article, media abstract, or text printout to find a word, name, date, phrase, idea, or general overview of the resource.	
2. Scan/search materials in electronic or other non-print formats.	
B. Conduct primary research as needed.	
1. Plan and complete an interview, experiment, or observation.	
2. Plan and conduct a survey/questionnaire.	

Information Literacy   149

Appendix B: Research Process Competencies: A Planning Guide

Competencies	Planning Space

9: EVALUATE, SELECT, AND ORGANIZE INFORMATION
 	
A. Screen the potential bits of information.
  1. Choose those that contribute to the search questions.
  2. Record the chosen information in an organized way.
B. Evaluate for currency of information.
  1. Identify copyright date.
  2. Identify the actual date, era, time period the ideas were created.
  3. Understand the significance of dated vs. current information, or whether dating is significant at all.
C. Establish authority.
  1. Identify the contributor/producer of the sources being used.
  2. Evaluate the contributor's/producer's work for motive, point of view, bias, scholarship, intended audience, etc.
D. Distinguish among fact, opinion, and propaganda.
E. Select information that is most useful in meeting the needs of the central question. Eliminate irrelevant information.	

Information Literacy

Appendix B: Research Process Competencies: A Planning Guide

Competencies

11: DETERMINE HOW TO USE/PRESENT/ COMMUNICATE INFORMATION; ORGANIZE INFORMATION FOR INTENDED USE; USE INFORMATION

A. Determine the most effective method of presentation.
   1. Identify and use appropriate media technologies.
   2. Consider presenting thoughts, feelings, and creative ideas through student-produced media: books, posters, transparencies, slide shows, puppets, audio and video tapes, hypermedia, etc.

B. Plan the project, e.g., dramatization, debate, writing, multimedia slide show, videotape presentation, demonstration, exhibit.
   1. Decide purpose; e.g., to inform, persuade, entertain, etc.
   2. Select an appropriate organizational style.
   3. Determine main points to be made or arguments to be developed and adapt working outline.
   4. Use the composition process; including prewriting, rough draft, writing/designing/ scripting, etc. (Most forms of presentation require some written planning.)

Planning Space

Information Literacy 153

Index

Academic achievement and collaboration, 38
Angiulo, Hilda, 55
Art as an information source, 62-63
Artifacts as an information source, 62-63
Audience - establishing an, 99-100
Authentic assessment, 46

Background - building of, 83-84
Bilingual specialists - as curricular planning team members, 30
Boolean logic, 96
Brainstorming, 81-82
Business education, 40

Casey, Beth, 78
Cole, Elizabeth Hartung, 3
Collaboration and academic achievement, 38
Collaborative data gathering, 67-68
Collaborative grouping, 101-3
Collaborative planning
    constructivist approach, 36-38
    constructivist method model, 37
    model of, 35
    traditional approach, 33-35
Community as an information source, 54-56
Community members - as curricular planning team members, 31
Comparing and contrasting, 89
Comprehensible input, 105
Computer information sources, 65-66.
Constructivist planning model, 37. *See also* Collaborative planning.
Consumer education, 41
Contextualization, 106
Contrasting and comparing, 89
Cooperative learning, 101-3
Critical thinking, 72
Culture and information, 3-4
Curricular partnership planning model, 35

Curricular planning team, 30

Engaging problems, 40-44
English as a second language specialists (ESL), 30-31
    as curricular planning team members, 30-31
English learners, 3-4, 69
    assistance from bilingual specialists, 30
    designing a mix for, 107
    SDAIE, 105, 127
English/language arts education, 42
ESL specialists - as curricular planning team members, 30-31
Evaluation of process, 27-28
Evaluation of product, 27-28

Gardener, Howard, 104
Goals 2000, 8
Gonzalez, Norma, 53
Gossard, Jenee, 97
Graphic organizers, 84-87

Health education, 43
Healy, Mary, 100
History education, 43
Home as an information source, 53-54
Homemaking education, 41

I-Search technique, 97-99
Ideas - organization of, 82-83
Industrial education, 44
Information
    analysis of, 26
    and culture, 3-4
    and language, 3-4
    communication of, 26-27
    integration of, 26
    interpretation of, 26
    need for, 21
    organization of, 25-26
    presentation of, 26-27
    relevance of, 25

    strategies for using, 24
Roth, Joyce, 125

Schifini, Alfredo, 81, 105-7
School as an information source, 56-58
Science education, 44
Science journaling, 75-76
Scientific thinking processes, 79-80
SDAIE, 105-7
Search process, 9, 11, 13-14, 19-28
Search questions
    formulation of, 21-22
    relationship to previous knowledge, 22
Search strategies - development of, 23
Searcher behaviors and competencies, 21-28
Searcher's thinking, 9, 10, 13-14
Searching, effective, 91-96
Series of events chain, 88
Sheltered English, 105-7
Short, Deborah, 77
Simulations, 68
Social science education, 43
Specially designed academic instruction in English (SDAIE), 105-7
Sternberg, Robert, 77, 78
Student learning
    facilitation of, 51
    tracking and assessment of, 51
Students, 31

Teachers - as curricular planning team members, 30
Teaching and learning - assessment of, 45-47
Teaching unit design, 38-39
Technology education, 44
Technology tools as an information source, 63-70
Telecommunications information sources, 66-67
Thinking, meaning-centered curriculum, 4-5
Time lines, 88
Tran, Mary, 86
Tucker, Edwin, 78

Unit design, 38-39

Venn diagrams, 89
Video technologies, 64-65

Watson, Clara Amador, 64
What Work Requires of Schools, 8
Writing - teaching of, 73-74

Yokota, Junko, 61